Letts STUDY GUIDE

AGE 11-14

KEY STAGE 3

GEOGRAPHY

Mike Clinch

- A clear introduction to the new National Curriculum

- Topic by topic coverage, with lots of diagrams and illustrations

- Frequent questions to test your knowledge

- Index and glossary of terms

First published 1992
Reprinted 1993, 1994, 1996
Revised 1995
Reprinted 1998 (twice), 1999, 2000, 2001 (twice), 2002

Letts Educational
The Chiswick Centre
414 Chiswick High Road
London W4 5TF
Tel: 020 8996 3333

Text: © Mike Clinch 1995

Illustrations: Ian Foulis Associates, Chris Evans, Goodfellow & Egan
©Letts Educational Ltd 1995

British Library Cataloguing in Publication Data
A CIP record for this book is available from the British Library

ISBN 1 85758 939 4

Acknowledgements
I would like to thank Peter Nash and his daughter Emily; Clwyd Jones and his
daughter Rachel, Nicholas Silverthorne, Steven Cameron; Denis Meadmore of Coed
Morgan Farm and the staff of the NRA (Monmouth) for their contributions. I would
also like to thank Angela Royal and Andrew Thraves for giving me the opportunity to
write this book. I am grateful to Richard Carr and Wayne Davies of Letts for their
support and guidance during the revision of this project. I am especially indebted to my
wife, Charmaine, for her patience, help and guidance. Without her this book would not
have been possible.

Mike Clinch

The author and publishers are grateful to the following for permission to reproduce
photographs and prints:

Aerofilms Ltd p108; The Channel Tunnel Group Limited p117; Bruce Coleman Limited
pp37, 38, 39, 40, 53, 64, 66, 68, 71, 78, 83, 90, 96, 97, 109, 110, 113, 123, 131, 132, 135, 139,
144, 145, 149; The Cheltenham Newspaper Co Ltd p72; DIAF Agence d'Illustration
Photographique pp38, 39, 40; The Environmental Picture Library: (Shahidul
Alam/Drik/CARE) p47, (Heidi Bradner) p145, (A Greig) p83, (J Holmes) p123, (Michael
McKinnon) p83, (V Miles) p83; Holt Studios International pp57, 72, 123, 147; Frank Lane
Picture Agency Ltd pp60, 61, 85, 94; London Transport Museum p9; Magnum Photos
Ltd (David Hurn) p141; Marion and Tony Morrison pp53, 54, 55, 57; The National
Meteorological Library pp90, 91; Ordnance Survey map extracts reproduced with the
permission of the Controller of Her Majesty's Stationery Office © Crown copyright
pp10, 17, 20, 21, 68, 74, 113; Science Photo Library pp60, 94, 125; Somerset County
Gazette p114; Tony Stone Images pp27, 47, 90, 131, 144; Ian Thraves Photography pp63,
64, 68, 69, 70, 71, 79, 110, 115, 118, 120, 125, 128, 129, 131, 139, 140; Topham Picturepoint
pp50, 84, 104, 145; Tony Waltham Geophotos pp47, 69, 70, 71; Woodmansterne Picture
Library, Photos © Woodmansterne pp68, 113.

Material from the National Curriculum is Crown copyright and is reproduced by
permission of the Controller of HMSO.

Grateful acknowledgement is also due to Exmoor National Park Authority and to
B T Batsford Ltd.

Every effort has been made to trace copyright holders and to obtain their permission for
the use of copyright material. The author and publishers will gladly receive information
enabling them to rectify any error or omission in subsequent editions.

Printed in Great Britain by Bath Press Colourbooks, Glasgow

Letts Educational Limited, a division of Granada Learning Limited. Part of the Granada PLC

Contents

*I*ntroduction

SUCCESSFUL STUDYING AT KEY STAGE 3

During Key Stage 3 of the National Curriculum, you will have to study the following subjects:

English, Mathematics, Science, Technology, a modern foreign language (usually French or German), Geography and History.

This stage of your education is very important because it lays the foundation for your GCSE courses. The National Curriculum requires you and all 11–14 year olds to follow the same programmes of study; these define the knowledge and skills you need to learn and develop during your course.

At school, your teachers will be monitoring your progress. At the end of Key Stage 3, your performance will be assessed and you will be given a National Curriculum level. Most students should reach level 5 or level 6, some may reach levels 7 or 8, or perhaps even higher. In English, Mathematics and Science, you will have to take a National Test towards the end of your last year at Key Stage 3. The results of your tests, also marked in levels, will be set alongside your teachers' assessment of your work to give an overall picture of how you have done.

How this book will help you

You should use this book at home to support the work you are doing at school. Think of it as a companion or study guide to help you prepare for class work and homework. Inside the book you will find the level descriptions which will be used to assess your performance. We have included them so that you will be able to check how well you are doing as you near the end of Key Stage 3.

Reading this book and doing the questions and activities will help you get to grips with the most important elements of the National Curriculum. Before you begin to read the book itself, take a few moments to read the introductory sections on 'Geography in the National Curriculum' and 'How to use this book'.

GEOGRAPHY IN THE NATIONAL CURRICULUM

Geography is about people and places. Geographers study how different people and different landscapes are affected by their natural and human environments. We are all geographers – some of us, perhaps, without realising it.

We are all concerned with issues that affect our lives. It may be something local such as the building of a new road by-pass, the redevelopment of town centre shopping or even something as simple as 'What is the weather like today?' It may be something on a regional scale, such as how the building of a new motorway will affect the region in which we live. Current national scale issues include the proposed changes in the European Union and how they will affect us in the UK. Global issues such as famine in Africa and global warming also affect the way in which we live our lives. The world around us is constantly changing – the study of Geography helps us to understand and explain these changes.

So, what kind of things will you be doing as you cover Key Stage 3 Geography? You should adopt an 'enquiry approach' to your study. Each topic or theme should be approached with a series of questions: *What and where is it? What is it like? How did it get like this? How and why is it changing? How will the changes affect the people living there, the landscape and the environment?*

Skills

You will learn the skills of the geographer, such as making accurate measurements of geographical features, extracting information from maps and graphs, and identifying and describing geographical patterns. In particular, you will make detailed observations of the weather and learn how to read and interpret all sorts of maps, including Ordnance Survey maps.

Places

You will study a number of different places. Your local area and the UK should be central to your study but you will also study a country in Europe as well as an economically developing country. Students in Wales will study 'Wales' as a country.

Themes – Physical

As well as places there are ten themes that should be studied. The Physical Geography themes include the study of earthquakes or volcanoes, processes that shape the land (such as rivers or coasts), a study of the weather and why it varies from place to place, and a study of one world vegetation type (such as, among others, the tropical rainforest or savanna grasslands).

Themes – Human

Themes in Human Geography include population distribution and change, settlement patterns and how they are changing, and the distribution and changes in one type of economic activity (such as a type of farming, or one specific industry or hypermarkets).

Themes – Environmental

Themes in Environmental Geography include how different environments are managed, how providing a reliable resource (such as water or energy) can affect the environment, and how human activity is affecting the planet as a whole.

The important thing to note though, is that each theme in Geography cannot be studied in isolation. Geography is an integrated subject, that means that all the components are linked together and a change in one area can cause a chain reaction which results in changes somewhere else in the environment.

Don't be too worried if some of these subjects are unfamiliar to you at the moment. The National Curriculum in Geography is designed so that as you progress through each Key Stage you will be given the opportunity: to improve your geographical knowledge, to develop the necessary geographical skills, to practise what has been learnt through fieldwork exercises, to gain in the understanding of the processes of geographical change, and to begin to appreciate and predict the implications of our constantly changing world. This book will help you as you learn.

Remember that Geography is all around us – decisions that we make today, collectively and individually, no matter how small and seemingly insignificant, can have far reaching effects. Good luck and enjoy Geography!

HOW TO USE THIS BOOK

This book is not intended to be a scheme of work. The book's content is laid out in the same order as the National Curriculum so the skills section comes first, followed by places, physical themes and human themes. Environmental themes are integrated throughout, although the majority do come towards the end of the book. Opportunities to practise geographical skills also occur regularly.

Each section of the book should be used, where necessary, to support school-based work. By doing this you will gain a wider perspective, use more case studies as examples, and therefore develop a deeper understanding of key geographical topics.

Each unit is made up of an explanatory text and a series of activities. These activities are found in the 'Now test yourself' boxes. You should read through the relevant section of text before attempting these activities. The answers to most activities will be found at the back of the book. The exceptions are those activities which are locally-based, as there is a large and unpredictable range of possible answers.

Fieldwork is an essential and integral part of the National Curriculum. Some suggestions for fieldwork topics and project-based work are provided at various points in the text. You are encouraged to investigate geographical issues further. You could of course design your own fieldwork enquiries.

It is hoped too, that parents will read through the book so that they can get a better understanding of what modern Geography is about, and so be in a position to help at any stage.

CHAPTER 1

*B*asic skills

WHAT IS GEOGRAPHY?

Geography is about people and places. The study of Geography allows us to explore different parts of the world, experience different environments and discover different cultures and different ways of life. It helps us understand how people adapt to living in different parts of the world and the effect people have on their environment.

Geography can be studied on a variety of scales. Local Geography can have a serious impact on our lives, for example, the building of a new by-pass. Global Geography deals with issues such as international trade or climatic change.

All of us are geographers! We all have an interest in what goes on around us – whether it be an environmental issue, changes in our town or the weather. Decisions that we make everyday can have far reaching effects on other people and the environment.

Geography can be split into three sections.

- **Physical Geography** is concerned with the 'natural environment', for example, weather and climate, the processes that shape the land (such as weathering and the work of rivers, ice and the sea), different vegetation patterns, and earthquakes and volcanoes.
- **Human Geography** studies people and the activities they are engaged in, for example, population, towns and cities, industry and agriculture, transport and shopping patterns.
- **Environmental Geography** is concerned with the impact that human activities are having on the natural environment. The most common topics under this heading include pollution and conservation.

It is important to realise that each of the three different parts of Geography are linked together. A change in one section can set off a chain reaction which can affect many other areas.

The basic tool of any geographer is a map.

WHAT IS A MAP?

However we choose to find out about an area it is highly likely that we would use a map at some stage. Maps are used by all types of people in their jobs (e.g. travel agents, estate agents, taxi drivers) and in their leisure time (e.g. ramblers, hikers, tourists). There are many different types of map. For example, there are street maps, road maps, Ordnance Survey maps and sketch maps. Ordnance Survey maps are very detailed, while sketch maps give only brief information about an area.

Sketch maps

A sketch map is the least accurate type of map because it only gives a rough idea of the distance between places. Sketch maps can be used to give someone directions when planning a route. The illustration overleaf is an example of a sketch map.

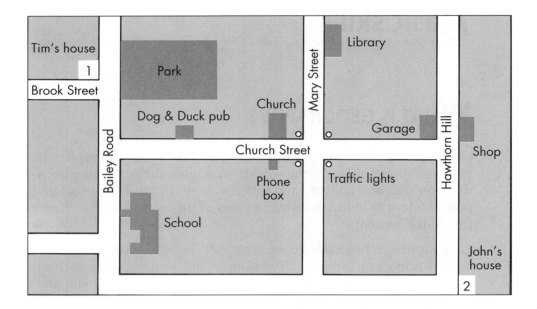

1 Tim intends to visit his friend John after school. He has to go home first to tell his parents where he is going and then return a library book before going on to John's house.
   Describe Tim's route from his house to John's house.

Plans

A plan is a drawing of something as seen from directly overhead. Plans may be used to give a bird's-eye view of buildings, parks, shopping centres, etc. The illustration shows a plan of a school.

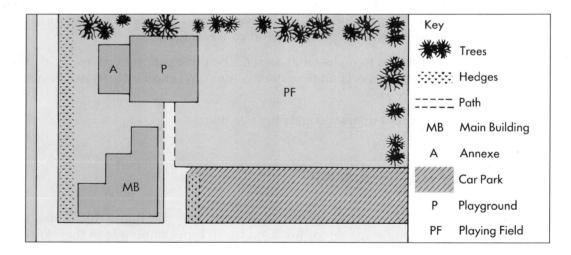

2 Your local newspaper is running a competition to design the layout for a new park in your community. The rules of the competition state that the park must include the following facilities: children's playground; adventure playground; duck pond; ornamental gardens and fountains; ice cream kiosks; paddling pool; picnic area; tennis courts; playing field; toilets; first aid station.
   Draw your competition entry using appropriate symbols and labels for your layout. Do not forget to include a key for your symbols.

Topological maps

A topological map shows a series of points or places in a sequence. It does not give accurate distances between places or the true direction. A good example is the London Underground railway system.

LRT Registered User No. 95/2236

Ordnance Survey maps

Maps produced by the Ordnance Survey (OS maps) show areas of the UK in great detail. Special skills are needed to be able to read and interpret them accurately.

Map symbols

It is not possible to label every feature included on a map. For this reason, signs and symbols are used to represent the various features we want to include on a plan or map. These symbols are then explained in a **key**. The symbols can be lines, small drawings, letters or coloured areas. Listed below are some of the symbols used on OS maps of the 1:50 000 series.

Lines	Small drawings	Coloured areas	Letters
Motorway	Bridge	National Trust (open all year)	P Post office
Main road	Golf course	(closed for part of year)	PH Public house
Secondary road	Three types of church	Wood	MP Mile post
Railway	Glasshouse	Park	CH Club house
Railway: single track	Tumulus	Orchard	TH Town hall
Railway stations	Triangulation pillar	Quarry	
Viaduct		Buildings	
Cutting		Lake	**Tourist information**
Embankment	Windmill		
Tunnel	Windpump	Beaches (sand) (shingle)	Information centre
Footpath	Coach station		Parking
National park boundary	Lighthouse		Picnic site
River	Beacon	Cliffs	Viewpoint
Pipeline	Battlefield		Campsite
Pylons	Spot heights	Spoil heap	Caravan site
Contours			Youth hostel

9

Scale and distance

One of the most important uses for a map is to show how far one place is from another. Scale allows us to do this.

The amount of detail shown on a map is also determined by the scale. A large scale map shows a small area in great detail. A small scale map shows a large area in less detail. If you wanted to find information about a village then a large scale map would be most useful. If you wanted to find information about a country, then it is better to use a small scale map. Scale can be expressed in three ways:

- As a linear (line) scale, e.g.
  ```
  0                    1 km
  ```
- As a statement, e.g. 4 cm = 1 km
- As a ratio, e.g. 1:25 000

Three maps of the village of Iford shown at different scales.

Map A (1:10 000)   **Map B** (1:25 000)   **Map C** (1:50 000)

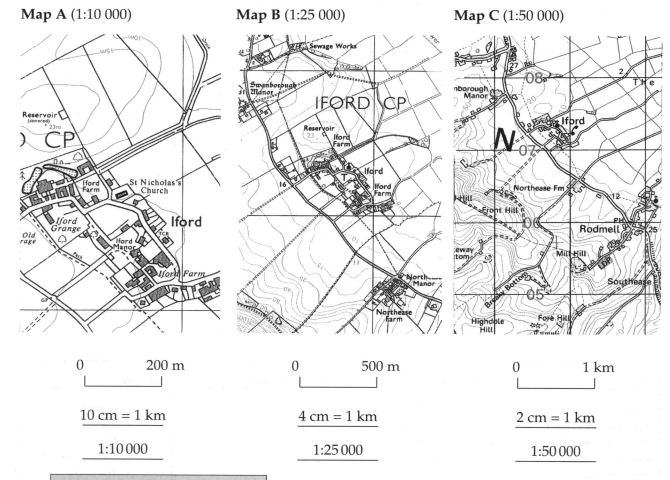

0 200 m	0 500 m	0 1 km
10 cm = 1 km	4 cm = 1 km	2 cm = 1 km
1:10 000	1:25 000	1:50 000

Now test yourself

3 Which of the maps above shows: (a) the greater area?
                                    (b) the village of Iford in most detail?

4 Study all three maps. What is the name of the church shown on both map B and map C?

5 Name two things shown on maps A and B but not on map C.

6 Give one reason why the features mentioned in question 5 are not shown on map C.

How to measure distances

Look at map B on the previous page. The scale is 4 cm = 1 km. This means that every 4 cm measured on the map represents 1 km on the ground, e.g.

A line measuring 6 cm:

$$(4 \text{ cm}) \ 1 \text{ km} \quad + \quad (2 \text{ cm}) \ ^1/_2 \text{ km} = 1 ^1/_2 \text{ km}$$

Now test yourself

7 What distance on the ground would these lines represent? Measure the lines and then look at the scale very carefully. Remember that scale can be written in three different ways. Answer in kilometres or metres.

Scale	
	(a) ——————————————————
4cm = 1km	(b) ————————————
	(c) —————
	(d) ————————————————————
1:50 000	(e) —————————
	(f) ———————————
	(g) —————————
0 100m	(h) —————
	(i) ———————

Grid references

Four figure grid references

To find places accurately, OS maps have a grid drawn on them. The grid is made up of a series of lines going up and down, as well as across the page. Each line has a number written at its end. The vertical lines are called **eastings** (numbers increase towards the east). The horizontal lines are called **northings** (numbers increase towards the north).

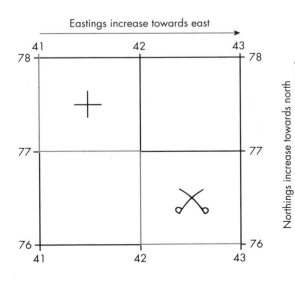

The **grid reference** of a square is described by these lines. The grid reference of the bottom left hand square on the grid opposite is 4176. This is because the easting '41' and the northing '76' cross in its left hand corner.

For example, the four figure grid reference for:

- the church (+) is 4177;
- the battlefield ($\times$) is 4276.

When reading grid references always remember an L shape and to write eastings before northings.

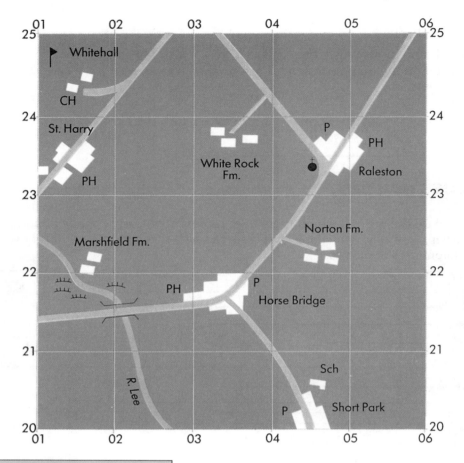

Now test yourself

8 Write down the names of the villages found in the following squares (where the buildings are, not where the name is written):
(a) 0423   (b) 0123   (c) 0420   (d) 0321

9 Give the four figure grid references for the squares in which the following symbols are found:
(a)   (b) Sch   (c)   (d)

10 Name two different buildings in:
(a) 0423   (b) 0420

11 Name the buildings in:
(a) 0422   (b) 0124   (c) 0122

Six figure grid references

A four figure grid reference is useful when finding a particular square on a grid. On OS maps of 1:50 000 and 1:25 000 series, a grid square represents a square kilometre. Sometimes greater accuracy than this is required when locating a specific point, such as a building or map symbol. In this case we use a six figure grid reference, which is accurate to within 100 square metres.

For example, to give the six figure grid reference for the youth hostel in square 4176:

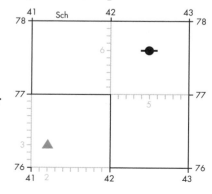

❶ read easting line '41' + two parts of the way towards line '42', so the first three numbers are 412;

❷ read northing line '76' + three parts of the way towards line '77', so the next three numbers are 763;

❸ therefore, the six figure grid reference is 412763.

See if you can work out why the six figure reference for the bus station is 425776.

Now test yourself

12 Use the map to complete the table. Remember, it is the centre of the symbol that gives the grid reference.

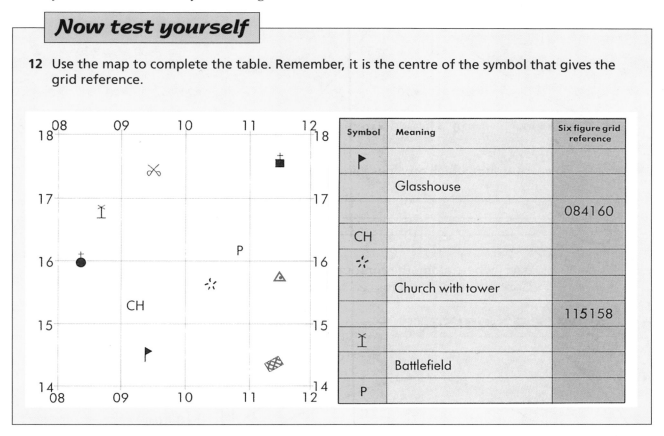

Symbol	Meaning	Six figure grid reference
⚑		
	Glasshouse	
		084160
CH		
☼		
	Church with tower	
		115158
⚒		
	Battlefield	
P		

Height on maps

The land around us is not flat like a piece of paper. So when a map is drawn, various methods are used to show the different heights of the land. These methods can tell us exactly how high a mountain is, as well as giving us an idea about the **relief** (shape of the land).

On a map, height may be shown by using:

• **colour or shading** so that different heights are shown by different bands of colour;

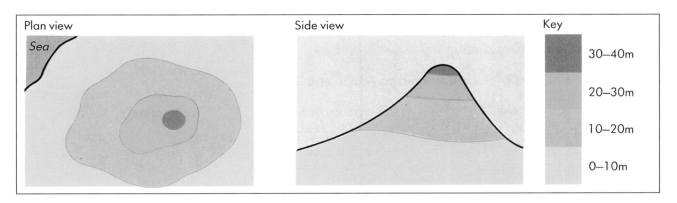

- **spot heights** which are dots on the map with a number next to them, the number indicates exactly the height of that point above sea level;

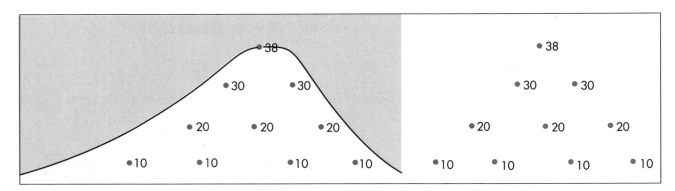

- **contours** which are lines joining places of the same height above sea level, e.g.

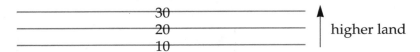

higher land

everywhere along the contour line marked '10' is 10 metres above sea level. Contour lines *never* cross each other!

Now test yourself

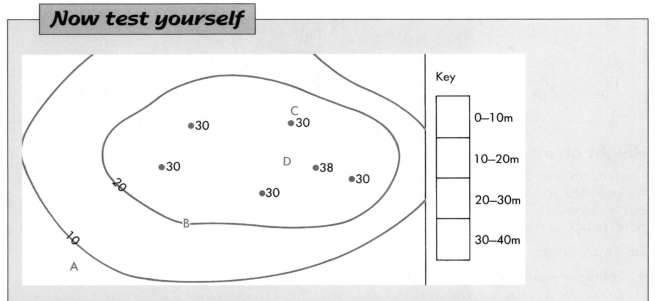

The diagram above shows an incomplete contour map. Trace the map before attempting the questions.

13 Complete the 30 m contour line.

14 Give the heights of the points marked A, B, C and D.

15 Using a graded colour scale, shade the map according to height and complete the key.

Using contour lines

In order to get a better idea of the shape of the land shown on an OS map, it is necessary to look carefully at the contour lines. The space between each line shows the distance on the land you would have to travel in order to gain 10 metres in height.

When contour lines are close together, the land is steeply sloping. When the contour lines are far apart, the land is gently sloping. If there are no contour lines then the land is flat.

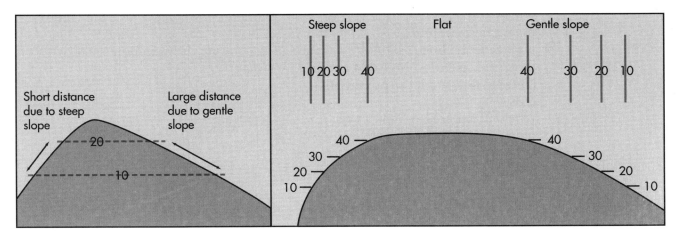

Contour patterns

Groups of contour lines drawn together make up a contour pattern which shows the shape of the land. Common landscape features have their own distinctive contour patterns. There are as many contour patterns as there are landscape features. Look at the contour patterns (note the height of each contour).

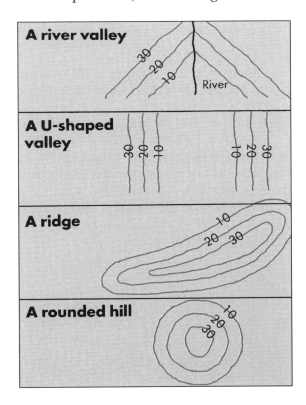

Drawing cross-sections

You can use contour lines to draw a **cross-section**. The contour lines on a map give the plan view. When you draw a cross-section you can see the shape of the land from the side. There are two methods of drawing a cross-section.

Method 1

❶ using a ruler, join the points A and B together with a line, this is your **line of section**;

❷ draw a graph frame below the contour map, it should be exactly the same width as the line A-B (the vertical scale should go from 0 to above the value of the highest contour);

❸ each time the line A-B on the map crosses a contour, draw a faint line down to the graph as far as the value of that contour, and mark the point with a cross;

❹ when all the crosses have been marked, join them up with a smooth curve (do not use a ruler) to show the outline of the land.

It may not always be possible to draw a cross-section in this way if there is not enough room beneath the contour map, or particularly if you want to transfer information from a map into your workbook.

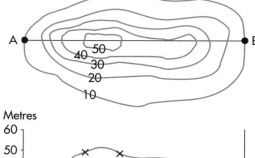

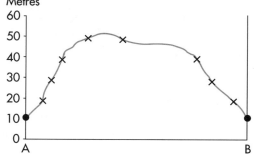

Method 2

❶ using a ruler, join the points A and B together to make your line of section;

❷ lay the edge of a piece of paper along the line of section, mark points A and B onto the paper edge;

❸ each time the line of section crosses a contour, mark it onto the paper edge with its height;

❹ draw a graph frame on which to draw the cross-section (step 2 in Method 1);

❺ place the edge of the paper along the base of the graph, and transfer the points and heights onto the base line;

❻ draw the faint lines upwards from the baseline and mark the points with a cross at the correct heights.

❼ join up the points with a smooth curve.

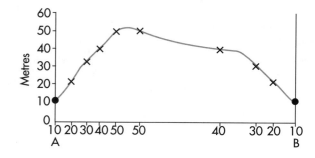

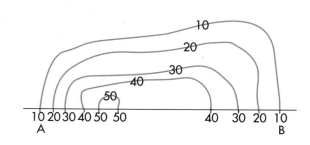

Now test yourself

16 Trace the cross section below and then complete it.

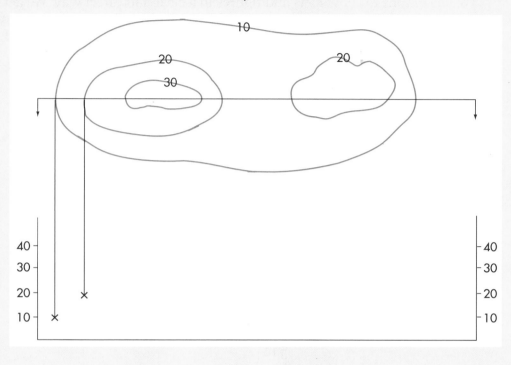

Now test yourself

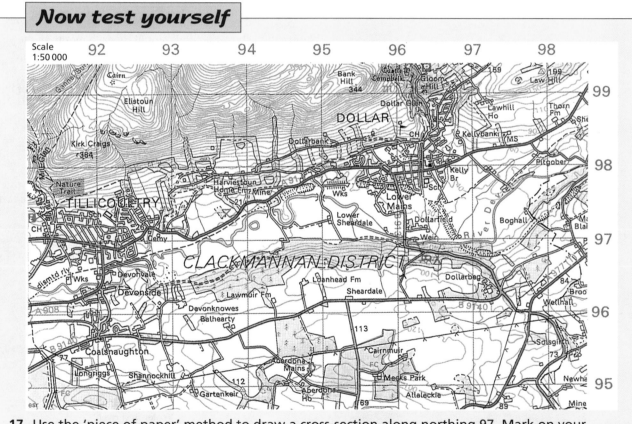

17 Use the 'piece of paper' method to draw a cross-section along northing 97. Mark on your cross-section three places where it crosses the river.

18 Match the grid square with the type of slope:
Gentle   Flat   Steep   9399   9597   9395

U SING GRAPHS

We use graphs to show facts and figures in a clear and direct way. We get a lot of information from studying the shape of a graph carefully. There are four main types of graph. It is important to choose the right kind of graph to show the information clearly.

- **Line graphs** show averages and how things change over time: the steeper the graph the greater the change (if the graph is flat then there is no change).

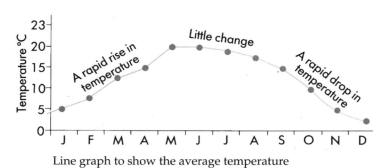

Line graph to show the average temperature

- **Bar graphs** show totals: the longer the 'bar' the greater the total.

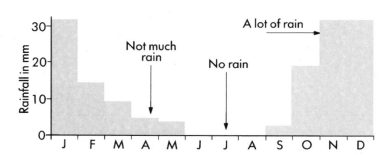

Bar graph to show the total rainfall for each month of the year

- **Pie charts** show percentages: the 360° in a circle equals 100%, so every 1% = 3.6° of the circle.

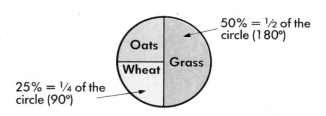

Pie chart to show the percentage of land used on a farm

- **Scattergraphs** show relationships: for example, what happens to water in a river as the rainfall changes?

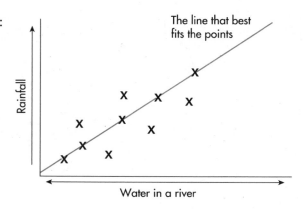

The scattergraph shows that as more rain falls, the amount of water in the river also increases.

Draw a graph for each of the four sets of figures outlined below. Choose the most appropriate forms of graph for each.

19 Percentages to show how people travel to work in a city centre office

Car	50%
Bus	20%
Train	25%
Walk	5%

20 The relationship between the number of cars in a city centre and the levels of pollution

Number of cars	Level of sulphur dioxide in parts per million
100	157
200	296
500	402
1000	536
1500	684

21 The total number of vehicles travelling down a main street in a day

am	Midnight	1	2	3	4	5	6	7	8	9	10	11	Noon
	20		15	5	3	5	10	20	50	140	120	100	70	80

pm	1	2	3	4	5	6	7	8	9	10	11	Midnight
	120	100	80	130	130	100	80	50	60	30	25	20

22 The total number of visitors to a tourist centre during each month of the year

J	F	M	A	M	J	J	A	S	O	N	D
20	15	40	100	500	1000	1100	1200	600	400	80	40

TEST YOUR MAP SKILLS

Following a route on a map

The idea of a treasure hunt is to follow a route on a map, and pick up the answers to questions on the way. Study the map on the next page.

23 Find the school in Pensford. Follow the main road south from the school.
   (a) How high is the first spot height you see?
   (b) Name the first hamlet you pass through.
   (c) Name the bridge at the crossroads.

24 Turn left at the crossroads.
   (a) In which direction are you now travelling?
   (b) Name two buildings in Chelwood.

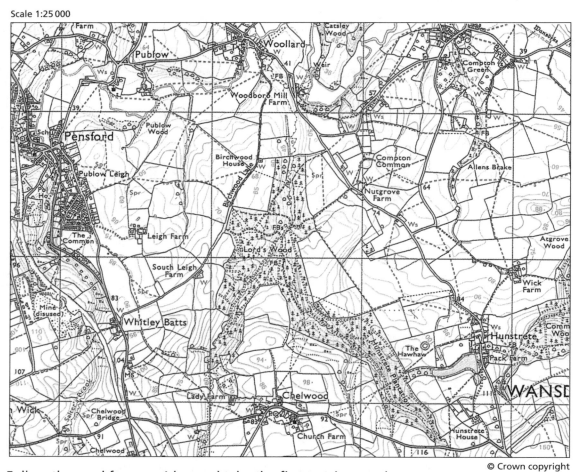

Scale 1:25 000

© Crown copyright

25 Follow the road for over 1 km and take the first turning north.
  (a) Name the first farm you pass through.
  (b) Name the area of woodland you can see to your left.

26 Follow the road as far as Woollard. Turn west just after the bridge.
  (a) For the first ½ km, are you travelling uphill or downhill?
  (b) To see the river would you have to look north or south?

27 Follow the road over the bridge. What is the first spot height you pass?

28 You want to get back to the school as quickly as possible.
  (a) At the junction do you:
      (i) turn right, then right again; (ii) turn right, then left; (iii) go straight on?
  (b) If you have taken the shortest route, have you travelled about 5 km, 10 km, 15 km or 20 km?

More map exercises

Study the map on page 21.

29 Name two different buildings found in the village of Llanfoist (2813).

30 Give the six figure grid reference of:
  (a) the coach station in Abergavenny.
  (b) the railway station in Abergavenny.
  (c) the 102m spot height on the A465(T) near Gilwern.
  (d) the highest part of Blorenge Mt., south-west of Abergavenny.

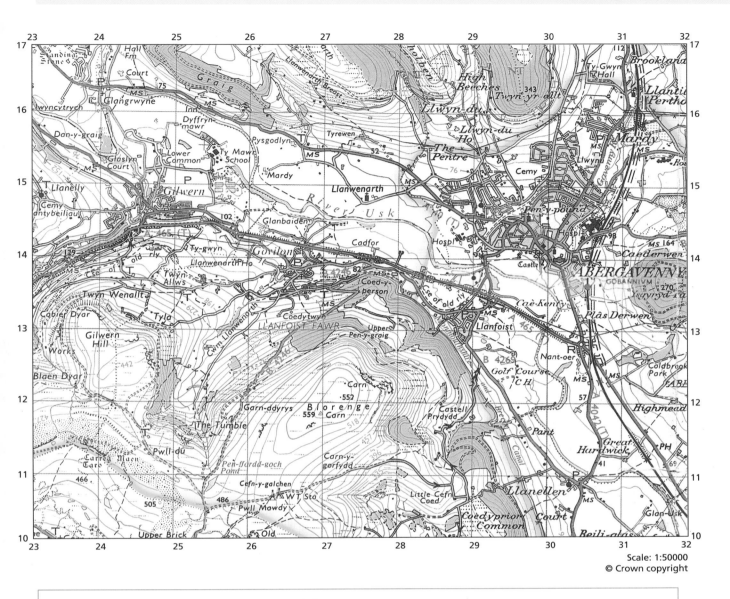

Scale: 1:50000
© Crown copyright

31 What is the straight-line distance in kilometres:
(a) from Llanwenarth Church (276148) to Ty Mawr School (256155);
(b) along the A465(T) from the roundabout in grid square (3012) to the roundabout in grid square (2514)?
(c) What is the actual distance along the river from the bridge at Glangrwyne (241161) to the bridge at grid reference (292139)?

32 Describe the shape of the land in each of these grid squares:
(a) 3111   (b) 2515   (c) 2712

33 You are a taxi driver who has been called to Abergavenny Hospital (3014). You are given a set of directions to follow to get your passenger home. Follow the instructions below to find where the passenger lives.
Come out of the hospital onto the B road and turn right towards Abergavenny town centre. At the junction of the main road turn left and then left again onto the A40(T). You should now be travelling in a generally southerly direction. At the roundabout take the A4042(T) and continue for about 2 km. Turn right at the first 'T' junction you come to, so that you pass a church with a spire. Your passenger lives behind the church. What is the name of the village?
If the taxi fare is £1 for every kilometre travelled, how much would the passenger have to pay?

CHAPTER 2

*P*laces – the local area and the United Kingdom

WHERE DO I LIVE?

The places in which people live all have names. When a place has a name it is easier to find it on a map. It is also easier to describe a location in relation to other places if it has a name. For example, every house or flat has an address so the letters and parcels can be delivered to the correct place.

Now test yourself

My address

1   Write your name.

2   Write your house number and street underneath.

3   Your street may be part of a larger area or district, write this underneath (if you live in a small town or village then you may not have a district).

4   Write your town underneath.

5   All towns are in a county. Write your county down next.

6   Write your postcode underneath.

7   Finally, write down the country you live in.

Case study: Stephen's street

Stephen lives in a small street in the village of Trelewis near Merthyr Tydfil in Mid Glamorgan, South Wales. Here is a plan of his street.

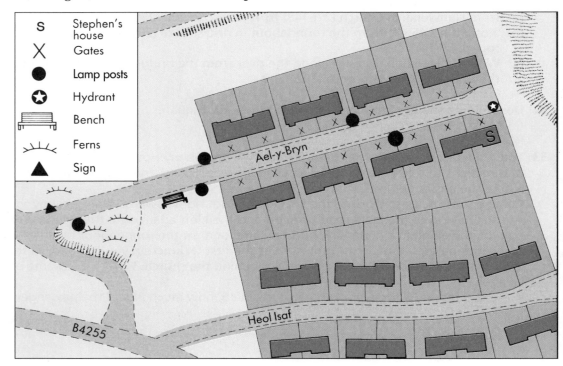

Now test yourself

Look at the plan opposite.

8   How many houses are there in Stephen's street?

9   What is the name of his street?

10 Stephen's street is a dead end. Do you think there will be a lot of traffic? Who would use his street?

11 Draw a sketch map of your street, or if you live in a long street just draw the section around where you live. Don't forget to add any lamp posts, public telephones and other features.

Now test yourself

Fieldwork/enquiry: street survey

12 Use the questionnaire outlined below to find out more about your street. Try to ask as many of your neighbours as you can. (Remember – always be polite when asking people questions.)

• Name and address of person interviewed.

• How long have you lived here?

• Do you know how the street got its name?

• Has anything changed in the street since you moved here?

• Are there any improvements you would like to see in the street?

Your local area

Your street is just a part of your local area. It is useful to know what the environment around us is like, and it is important to know where to find certain places.

Questions to ask ourselves about our local area could include:

• Where is the nearest bus stop or railway station?
• What is the way to school?
• Where is the nearest park or youth club?
• How far is it to my best friend's house?
• Which way are the shops?
• Can I walk to the local sports centre, or is it too far?

Now test yourself

Look at the sketch map opposite.

'I go out of school and turn left. I walk along Coronation Street and I can see some swings on my left. To my right is the park, with trees and a duck pond in it. Next I turn left into Ramsey Street and I can see the shop on my right. I walk past my neighbour's house and I am home.'

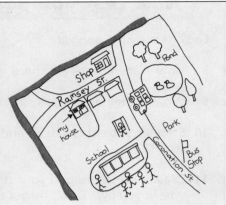

Take a look at the streets where you live. Make a note of the places or buildings you could put on a map. Don't forget your own house.

13 Draw a rough map first and then, when you are happy with it, make a neat copy. Colour in your map.

14 Describe in words a route you would take from your house to one of the buildings you have drawn, or you could describe your route to school.

THE BRITISH ISLES: COUNTRIES AND CITIES

The United Kingdom is made up of four countries – England, Scotland, Wales and Northern Ireland. Each of these countries has its own capital city although there is only one central government, based in London.

Political maps show countries, cities, main roads and other 'human features'.

Letter-number co-ordinates are used on some maps to find places more accurately. For example, on the map opposite co-ordinate A1 is clearly marked.

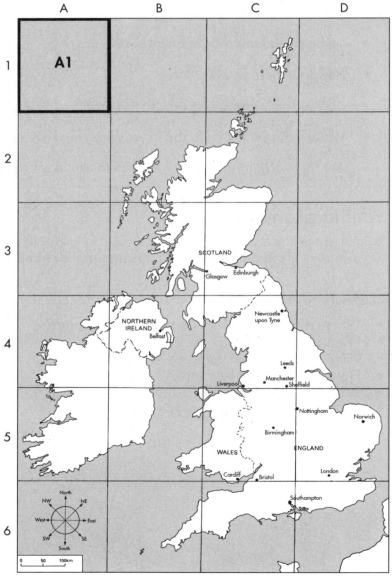

A political map of the British Isles

Now test yourself

Look at the map on page 24.

15 Name the cities in each of these squares:
(a) B4   (b) C6   (c) C3

16 Give the co-ordinates for:
(a) Norwich   (b) Liverpool   (c) Cardiff

17 Which co-ordinate has the most number of cities?

Answer these questions using the compass and the map on page 24.

18 Leeds is south of _____ .

19 Glasgow is _____ of Edinburgh.

20 Birmingham is north west of _____ .

21 Cardiff is _____ of Birmingham and west of _____

22 _____ is south-west of London.

23 Using a political map of Britain in an atlas, locate approximately where you live.

24 Describe your location using the words country, region, county and town.

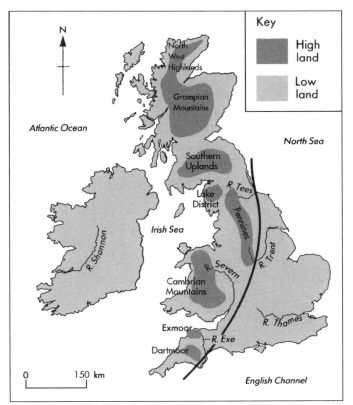

A physical map of the British Isles

Physical maps show mountains and rivers and other 'natural features'.

Britain on a physical map can be divided into highland Britain and lowland Britain by an imaginary line, joining the mouth of the River Exe in Devon with the mouth of the River Tees in Cleveland. To the north and west of this line the rocks are very old, very hard and therefore form mountains. To the south and east of the line the rocks are much younger, softer and have therefore been eroded into lowlands.

Now test yourself

Using a physical map in your atlas:

25 Find the highest points of the mountains labelled on the physical map on page 25.

26 In which mountains do the following rivers start and into which seas do they flow?
Mersey   Clyde   Tyne

27 Name four groups of islands found around the coastline of Britain.

In which region do you live?

The United Kingdom can be divided into a number of regions. A region is a large area of the country, made up of a number of counties. Usually there is one large city in each region, but larger regions can have more than one city and many large towns. Sometimes there are no definite boundaries to regions. One person's idea of what that region is can be different from their neighbour's, so general terms such as 'South East', or 'East Midlands', are used to describe regions.

Regions of the British Isles

Now test yourself

How to find out the name of the region in which you live.

28 What is the name of your local:
(a) Water Company   (b) TV station?

29 In which county do you live?

30 Using the map on page 26, and an atlas, name the counties which surround your county.

31 Name the region in which you live.

Images of different regions

Local areas within regions can vary enormously. Some of us live in the countryside, some in a town. Some of us live in large cities. Some people live on modern housing estates – others live in older houses in old industrial regions.

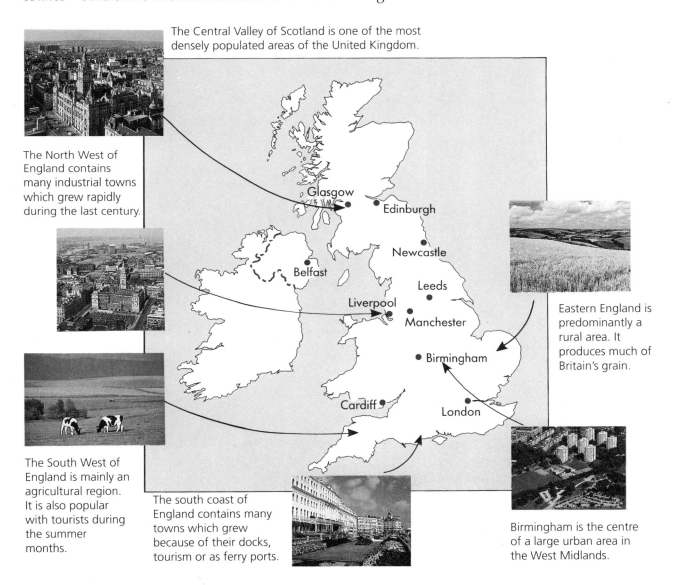

The Central Valley of Scotland is one of the most densely populated areas of the United Kingdom.

The North West of England contains many industrial towns which grew rapidly during the last century.

Eastern England is predominantly a rural area. It produces much of Britain's grain.

The South West of England is mainly an agricultural region. It is also popular with tourists during the summer months.

The south coast of England contains many towns which grew because of their docks, tourism or as ferry ports.

Birmingham is the centre of a large urban area in the West Midlands.

Glasgow
Edinburgh
Newcastle
Belfast
Leeds
Liverpool
Manchester
Birmingham
Cardiff
London

What is your image of places?

32 We all have ideas about what places are like. Sometimes our image of a place is totally inaccurate and bears no resemblance to what that place is really like. Our perceptions (how we see things) of a place are built up from pictures we see and stories we hear about that place.

For the following places, write down one word or phrase which comes into your mind that best describes your image of that place or the people that live there. Compare your comments with those of a friend or adult.

If you know someone who lives in a different part of the country, contact them and see what they think. Are their thoughts different to yours?

Scotland   Wales   Cornwall   Oxford   Northern Ireland   The Midlands   London   Newcastle

Wales

Wales is a country of contrasts.

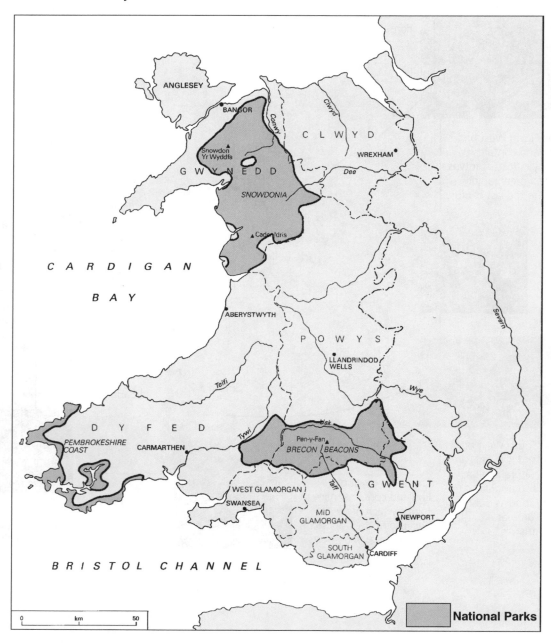

The Valleys

Much of south-east Wales, commonly known as 'The Valleys' were once dominated by heavy industry, such as coal mining and iron and steel production. Many millions of migrants were attracted to the area during the nineteenth century with the promise of jobs in the mines. Communities grew rapidly and the characteristic settlement pattern of terraced houses grew up along the valley sides. For over a century, the Welsh Valleys produced high quality coal that was exported all over the world. The struggle of their daily life, based on working 12 hours a day and chapel on Sundays, built a strong sense of community which still exists today.

Today the mines have all closed. The area qualifies for special assistance grants as high unemployment and low living standards are common. Many people have moved away to look for work, so an increasingly elderly population is left behind.

Cardiff

Cardiff was rated the third most-desirable city in Britain in which to live in a recent survey. It is now a major centre of industrial growth. The proximity of the M4 motorway and the Cardiff Bay scheme (see page 116) have all helped attract new industry. Cardiff is continually developing its already excellent shopping facilities. There are many theatres, cinemas and restaurants and its status as a capital city helps attract many tourists. There are even plans for Cardiff to build its own opera house.

Rural Wales

The counties of Powys in mid Wales, Gwynedd in the north, and much of Dyfed in the south-west are mountainous with steep, rugged hills. The climate is harsh with cool summers and cold winters, and the rainfall is high in all seasons. This sparsely-populated region lacks good communication links: major roads are few, there is no direct rail-link between north and south Wales, and bus services are infrequent. This is predominantly a farming area. Farmers' incomes are supplemented in summer with the many tourists that visit the area. They are attracted to the three National Parks (Brecon Beacons, Snowdonia, and the Pembrokeshire Coast) and other areas of outstanding natural beauty.

North-east Wales

This is also an industrial area of Wales. Population density is high, although parts of this area too, have suffered from large-scale industrial closure in recent years. However, this area is more closely-linked with the industrial areas of the Merseyside, Cheshire and the Midlands, rather than with the rest of Wales. This is due to the main communication routes through Wales which run from east to west, rather than north to south, because of the highland in mid Wales.

CHAPTER 3

Places – the wider world

P HYSICAL FEATURES OF THE WORLD

Now test yourself

You will need a blank physical map of the world (as below) and an atlas.

1   Find a physical map of the world in your atlas. On your blank map mark on the following features:
   (a) Sea areas: Pacific Ocean, Indian Ocean, North Atlantic Ocean, South Atlantic Ocean, Southern Ocean, Arctic Ocean, Caribbean Sea.
   (b) Mountain ranges: Rockies, Andes, Himalayas.
   (c) Rivers: Mississippi, Amazon, Nile, Ganges, Yangtze.

2   Join up each of the latitude lines marked. Label each line correctly with one of the following: Equator, Tropic of Capricorn, Tropic of Cancer, Arctic Circle, Antarctic Circle.

3   Name one mountain range that runs across the Equator.

4   What is the International Date Line?

5   What is significant about daylight hours at the Arctic and Antarctic Circles?

6   Which two seas are linked with (a) the Panama Canal (b) the Suez Canal?

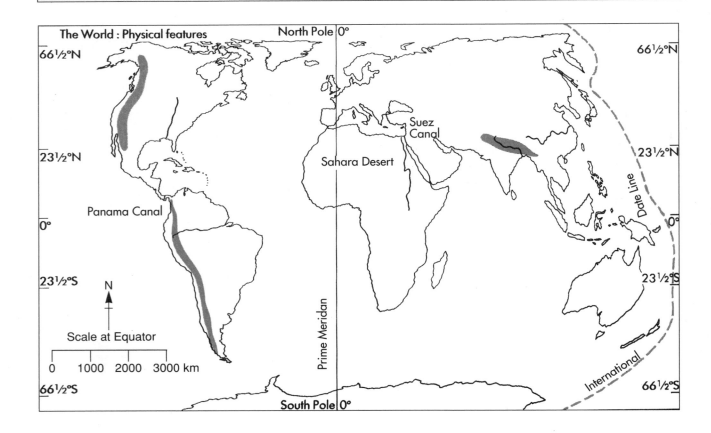

Now test yourself

You will need a blank political map of the world (see below) and an atlas.

7   On your blank map label the following continents:
    Africa; Europe; Asia; North America; South America; Oceania.

8   Use your atlas to locate the following countries, then shade them lightly on your blank map
    and correctly label them:
    Japan; Australia; South Africa; USA; Canada; Mexico; Brazil; Argentina; Venezuela; India;
    Bangladesh; China; Nigeria; Italy; Germany; France.

9   Each of the black dots on the map is one of the world's major cities. Use your atlas to label
    these cities correctly:
    Beijing; Sydney; Moscow; Tokyo; New York; Los Angeles; Mexico City; Cairo; Bombay;
    Buenos Aires.

10 Each of the stars on the map has a number. Join the stars using a black pen. Write above the
    completed line 'Developed North' and below the line write 'Developing South'.

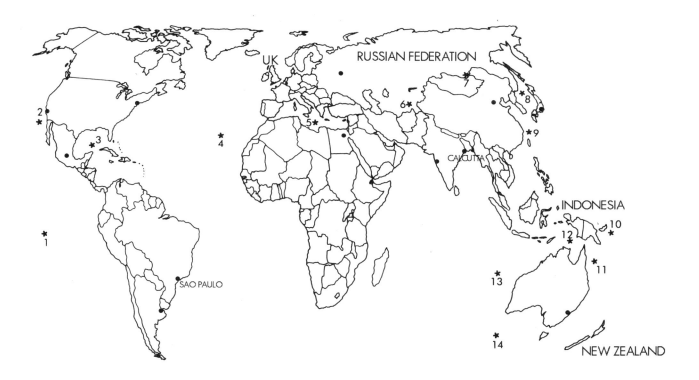

ALL COUNTRIES ARE NOT THE SAME!

Some countries are much richer than others. We can work out how rich or how
poor a country is by looking at how much the people earn, how many things they
own, how much they eat, how many of the children go to school and how healthy
the population is.

Wealthy countries are rich because they have **developed** their resources. They have
spent their money on building good schools, good roads and investing in health
care. Poor countries are poor because they are still **developing** their resources. They
find it very difficult to get enough money to build good schools, build good roads
and develop an efficient health service.

A five stage model has been put forward to help explain how the level of development increases.

Stage 1: Low levels of technology (machinery) and little capital (money) mean that raw materials are not developed, so there is very little industry or services.

Stage 2: An increase in the level of technology means that some primary raw materials (resources) can be exploited and are usually exported.

Stage 3: Levels of technology rise significantly and capital is more readily available, which enables manufacturing industries to grow. Factories require a transport system. Standard of living rises rapidly as country people move into the towns.

Stage 4: The rise in technological development increases. Fewer people are employed in primary activities. The service sector grows rapidly. Towns and cities continue to grow and so does the standard of living.

Stage 5: Service industries continue to grow, eventually employing more people than primary and secondary industry put together. A fourth type of economic activity has now developed – quaternary activity. Standards of living are very high compared with other stages.

Characteristics of developed and developing countries

Developed Countries	Developing Countries
Found in Europe, North America, Oceania and includes Japan.	Found in Asia, Africa, and South America.
Slow population growth due to low birth rates and low death rates.	Rapid population growth due to high birth rates and falling death rates.
Many doctors, nurses and hospitals.	Few doctors, nurses and hospitals.
Tertiary activity dominates the economy so wealth is generated.	Primary activities dominate so little wealth is generated.
Invest in developing countries and so earn interest on loans.	Owes money to countries in the developed world.
High standards of living.	Low standards of living.
Literacy rates quite high.	Literacy rates low.
Good nutritional levels.	Poor nutritional levels.
Dense road and rail networks.	Few roads and railways.

Indicators of how developed a country is include:

- **gross national product (GNP)** is the total value of everything produced in that country, when divided by the number of people living in that country it gives an indication of how wealthy people are;
- **life expectancy** is how long people in that country are expected to live;
- **infant mortality** is the number of babies who die before their first birthday;
- **people/doctor ratio** is the total number of people divided by the number of doctors, it gives an indication of how quickly you would be able to see a doctor if you were ill;
- **literacy rate** is the percentage of the population who can read and write.

	France	**Brazil**	**Bangladesh**
Status	Rich	Middle Income	Poor
GNP per head (£)	9183	1354	104
Life expectancy	74 yrs	65 yrs	51 yrs
Infant mortality	8/1000	63/1000	135/1000
People/doctor ratio	349	2402	10 925
Literacy rates	98%	76%	29%

Now test yourself

11 Find a map of the world in an atlas and locate the three countries listed in the table above.

12 You will need to look at all the information in the table to answer the following questions:
   (a) In which country do people live the longest? Suggest three reasons why this might be so.
   (b) Suggest two reasons why infant mortality rates are so high in Bangladesh.
   (c) People being able to read and write is very important if a country wishes to improve the overall standard of living. Why do you think this is so?

The jobs that people do in a country can be divided into four types of **economic activity**:

- **primary activity** is concerned with extracting or using natural resources, e.g. forestry, mining, farming and fishing;
- **secondary activity** is concerned with making things in factories (**manufacturing**) or putting parts together in **assembly plants** to form finished products, e.g. cars;
- **tertiary activity** is concerned with offering a service, e.g. a bank, a teacher, or transport;
- **quaternary activity** is concerned with new high-tech information services, research and development and advertising.

The percentage of the workforce employed in each activity gives a good indication of how developed a country is.

France

Much of French agriculture is modernised using fertilisers and machinery. People do not have to grow their own food – they can afford to buy it. They are then free to do other jobs.

Total population: 57 million
Percentage under 10 years old: 14.4%

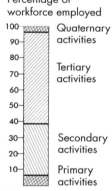

Percentage of workforce employed

Quaternary activities
Tertiary activities
Secondary activities
Primary activities

Brazil

Brazil borrowed a lot of money in the 1970s from the World Bank to build factories. Many people moved from the countryside to the towns in order to look for jobs. Many people are still employed in the primary activities, as Brazil has yet to develop fully its vast resources found in rainforest areas.

Total population: 158 million
Percentage under 10 years old: 25.4%

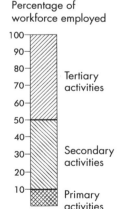

Percentage of workforce employed

Tertiary activities
Secondary activities
Primary activities

Bangladesh

Many people in Bangladesh have no income with which to buy food. There are few factories in Bangladesh.

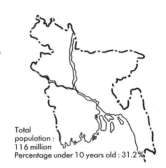

Total population : 116 million
Percentage under 10 years old : 31.2%

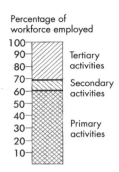

Percentage of workforce employed

Tertiary activities

Secondary activities

Primary activities

Now test yourself

13 Copy the table. Place each of the following statements under the correct heading.

Many employed in agriculture.
Few employed in agriculture.
Factories need a lot of workers.
Factories use machines for the jobs.
Many people employed in tertiary activities.
Fewer people employed in tertiary activities.

Farming is very primitive, using the simplest of tools.
Farming is advanced, using modern machines and fertilisers.
Factory workers work long hours for low wages.
Factory workers work for a set time and set wage each week.

Developed country	Developing country

Development and independence

The relationship that exists between wealthy developed countries and poorer developing countries and their trade links, are very important in determining how quickly a developing country increases its wealth. Economic growth is how quickly a country is raising its living standards. The rate of economic growth of a developing country depends on the natural resources available and how these are exploited. Many poorer developing countries do not have the technology, the skilled labour or the capital to develop their natural resources (whether the raw materials are mineral wealth or agricultural products) and so rely on the help of wealthy developed countries. The developing countries sell their raw materials on the world market at the lowest possible price. The raw materials are processed and manufactured in the wealthier developed countries and the consumable goods (what people buy in shops) are sold back to the poorer developing countries at a high price. This current state of international trade means that developing countries have even less money to develop their natural resources. It is a vicious circle of underdevelopment.

Places in the Developed World: Europe

The map of Europe has changed dramatically over the past few years. The break-up of Eastern Europe has seen the reappearance of many independent states. For example, East Germany and West Germany have united to form Germany, the former Yugoslavia has now broken up into six separate states, Czechoslovakia has divided into Slovakia and the Czech Republic, the Russian Federation is now made up of 14 states.

Although the people in some parts of Europe are not as well-off, most countries of Europe enjoy a high standard of living. On average, Europeans are much wealthier than most people in Africa, Asia and South America. This is because the economies of European countries are better developed than many parts of the world.

Now test yourself

14 Find a map of Europe in an atlas and look at the map on page 35.

(a) Name the *countries* marked Ⓐ, Ⓑ, Ⓕ, Ⓘ, Ⓟ and Ⓢ.

(b) Name the *cities* marked A, B, L, O, D and K.

(c) Name the *rivers* marked D and R.

CHAPTER 4

Places in the developed world

C ASE STUDY: FRANCE

France is the largest country in the European Community – it is almost twice the size of the UK. It has a total population of about 57 million (slightly less than the UK).

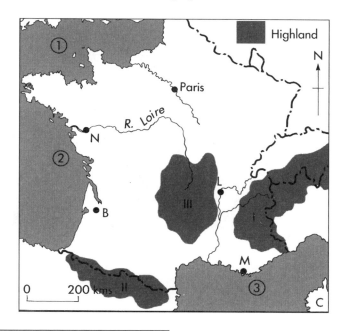

Now test yourself

Find a map of France in an atlas and look at the map above.

1 Name the sea areas marked ①, ② and ③.

2 Name the island marked C.

3 Name the cities marked B, L, M and N.

4 Name the rivers that flow through: (a) Paris; (b) city L.

5 Name the highland areas marked I, II and III.

Contrasts in France

France has a tremendous variety of landscape. The north coast is very different from the south coast. Brittany in the north-west is very different from Alpine France in the south-east. There is also a great variety of peoples, cultures and traditions. People of the French countryside are very different from the modern, fashion-conscious people of Paris.

Brittany is a part of France which has a history and culture all its own. The area was originally settled by Celts – the same people who settled in Ireland, Scotland and Wales. They even have their own language – Breton. The houses and buildings are very different in style from other parts of France.

Paris is one of the world's leading cities. It is a wealthy city, famous for its shops and its fashion. Tourists are attracted to its many historical and cultural sites. Paris has a reputation for being Europe's most romantic city.

The Massif Central is one of the poorer areas of France. It is a mountainous region where many people work on farms. Farming is difficult due to the steep slopes and poor soils, and because of this many people have left farming and have moved to other parts of France.

The French Alps for many years had few visitors. It was a poor region and the few people who lived there earned their living through dairying. Nowadays the Alps have become a major centre for tourism. During the winter skiers flock there in their thousands and during the summer people are attracted to the mountains for the scenery and fresh mountain air.

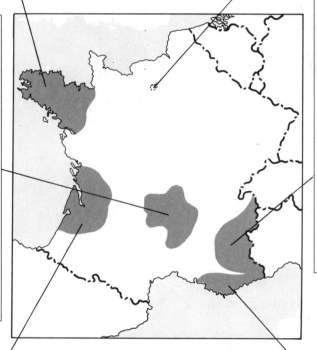

The South-west part of France is flat and has an ideal climate for growing grapes. It is one of France's most important wine-producing regions. Bordeaux wines are famous throughout the world, and so too is cognac, which is also produced in this region.

The French Riviera is one of the 'playgrounds of the rich'. The warm summer climate and the beaches of the Mediterranean attract some of the wealthiest people in the world. It is commonplace to see large expensive boats moored in the many marinas along the coast.

A game of boule in the late afternoon

Street cafe in Paris

Now test yourself

6   Which of the regions of France shown on the previous page is likely to be:
    (a) the wealthiest; (b) the poorest? Say why in each case.

7   More foreign visitors go to France than to any other country in Europe. List the attractions
    each of the six regions would have for the tourist.

Paris: a closer look

Paris was originally situated on an island in the middle of the river Seine – an important defensive site. Over the centuries, the city has grown steadily and is now home to over nine million people. Paris has become so important to France that it now dominates many aspects of French life.

Paris is the centre of the French government.

Paris is the main area for French industry, especially cars, chemicals and electrical goods.

With a population of nearly 9½ million, Paris is 8 times larger than any other French city.

Most large companies have their headquarters in Paris.

Paris is the main commercial and financial centre of France.

Paris is a main centre for the arts and entertainment, including the main TV stations.

With 12 universities Paris has 35% of all French students.

All railways and motorways lead to Paris.

Traffic congestion in Paris

The reason why traffic is a problem in Paris is that:

- Paris has over one million cars with only 720 000 parking spaces;
- thousands of buses and lorries use Paris streets every day;
- Paris streets are old and narrow, so traffic easily becomes congested;
- fumes and noise lead to high levels of pollution.

The possible solutions to the traffic congestion are to:

- build more motorways around the edge of the city;
- employ more tow trucks to remove illegally parked cars;
- issue drivers with special parking permits;
- restrict the number of cars on the road by using a number plate system – odd numbers one day, even numbers the next.

Now test yourself

8   Why was it originally important for Paris to be built on an island?

9   (a) List three ways in which Paris dominates French life.
     (b) What problems do you think this may cause the rest of France?

10   Look at each of the possible solutions to traffic problems above. Each one could create more problems than it solves. List the problems each solution would cause.

The Massif Central: a closer look

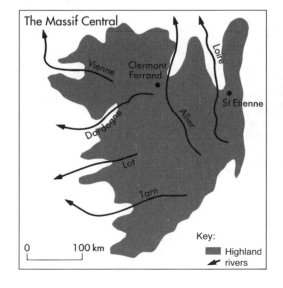

Clermont Ferrand

The Massif Central is a mountain region found in south central France. It is a farming region with some good land, but most of it is poor with thin soils, steep slopes and high mountains. Most of the farms are small and isolated and run by families. On the farms sheep and cattle are kept in small numbers.

The largest town in the region is Clermont Ferrand. It is a major centre for industry – the Michelin Tyre Factory employs nearly 18 000 people. The town attracts many young people from the surrounding countryside looking for work. St Etienne is also an industrial centre, although its importance is declining.

The Massif Central has these problems:

- it is high, rugged and isolated in many places, with heavy snow during the winter;
- farming is primitive and costly, and so products are not as cheap as those produced on efficient lowland farms;
- there are no facilities for young people, such as discos and cinemas;
- farming is difficult, so the farmers have to work hard for little profit;
- there are no jobs for young people, so they are forced to move out to places like Clermont Ferrand or even Paris;
- many of the farms and villages are becoming abandoned.

The government could develop the Massif Central in several ways:

- the farms could be joined together to make larger, more economical, more efficient units;
- more jobs could be provided for the young in forestry, craft and tourist industries;
- better houses could be built to encourage young people to stay;
- services could be improved with better roads and rail links;
- abandoned farms could be turned into holiday cottages and second homes;
- the area has been designated a National Park and tourism could be encouraged.

Now test yourself

11 Why is farming not as profitable on farms in the Massif Central as on lowland farms?

12 Why do you think there are so few towns in the Massif Central?

13 (a) List the reasons why young people are forced to move out.
   (b) What are the attractions of places like Clermont Ferrand for young people?

14 Why would the government want to encourage people to stay in the area?

15 Renovating old barns and farm buildings is not an ideal solution for the economy of the area. Why is this so?

France in the Modern World

The role of France in the modern world is varied. In terms of its importance as a world power, France ranks highly. It is an important member of NATO and also the UN Security Council. It is a founder member of the European Community and is strongly in favour of greater European unity. France also has strong links with countries outside Europe due to its colonial past.

France is renown the world over for being one of the major centres for fashion, for example, Chanel and Yves St Laurent. French food is also famous, particularly its wines and cheeses. France is an attractive tourist destination, catering for every type of tourist: art and fashion in Paris, family entertainment at Disneyland Paris, skiing in the Alps and Pyrenees, the beautiful south of France with its beaches and marinas, and the various regions within France that tempt with picturesque scenery and delicious local delicacies.

CASE STUDY: JAPAN

Industry in Japan

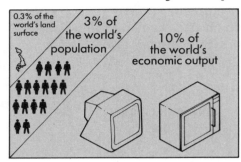

Facts and images of Japan

Japan is a remarkable country.

- in 1945 it was totally devastated after World War II;
- it has very few raw materials of its own;
- it has no oil and very little of other energy resources;
- it is a mountainous country with only 14% of its land flat enough to build on.

Yet despite all these problems, Japan is one of the world's leading industrial nations today.

In 1992 Japan:

- produced more cars than any other country in the world;
- produced 15% of the world's steel;
- launched more ships than anyone else;
- produced more televisions and radios than the whole of Europe;
- produced more watches than Switzerland;
- produced more high quality cameras than Germany;
- made significant advances in computer technology and is a world force in the aircraft and space industries.

Industrial areas of Japan

Most of Japanese industry is found around the coast, close to the main cities. This is mainly because Japan is heavily dependent on imported raw materials. The shallow bays and sheltered inlets offer ideal locations for ports. Many of the large factories are built on flat land reclaimed from the sea. It is easier to reclaim land when the sea is shallow.

The huge Mazda car factory built on reclaimed land

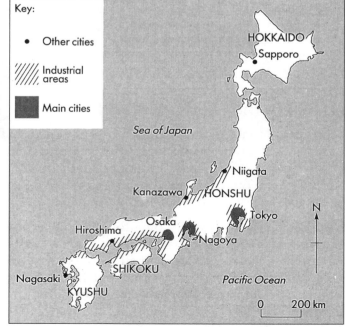

Key:

- • Other cities
- ///// Industrial areas
- ■ Main cities

Now test yourself

Use an atlas or the map on the previous page.

16 Copy and complete these sentences:
   (a) Japan is made up of many islands. The four main islands are _____ ;
   (b) Japan is part of the continent of _____ ;
   (c) The capital city of Japan is _____ .

17 List four things that can be bought in British shops that are made by Japanese companies.

18 (a) Find these Japanese companies hidden in the word square;
   Suzuki, Toyota, Honda, Sharp, Sanyo, Nikkon, Yamaha, Sony, Hitachi.
   (b) What sort of things does each company make?

H	N	I	K	K	O	N
U	I	U	P	H	A	S
Z	S	T	S	Y	D	U
S	S	O	A	Z	N	Z
H	A	Y	N	C	O	U
A	N	O	Y	Y	H	K
R	S	T	O	M	K	I
P	Y	A	M	A	H	A

19 Give two reasons why Japanese industry has developed along the coast.

20 Suggest two reasons why Japanese companies have become so successful.

Japan and international trade

Japan has few natural resources itself so it relies heavily on importing all its fuel and raw materials. But the Japanese people are very skilful in turning those imported raw materials into high quality manufactured goods. Japanese workers are so good at making things that Japan has a very favourable balance of trade – this means that the total value of exports is greater than the total cost of imports.

Product	In millions of dollars	
	Cost of imports	Value of exports
Food	14.4	0.7
Tea/coffee	0.7	–
Fuels and minerals	29.4	0.3
Chemicals	7.4	4.5
Manufactured goods	16.6	22.8
Machinery and transport	10.1	70.0
Total of all goods and services	126 408	209 151

(*Source: Geographical Digest, 1990–1*)

Where do Japan's imports come from?

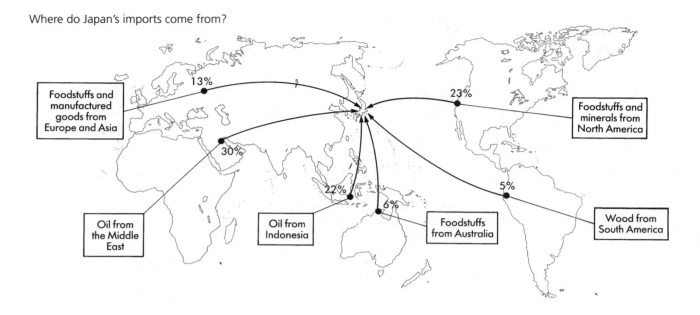

Where do Japan's exports go?

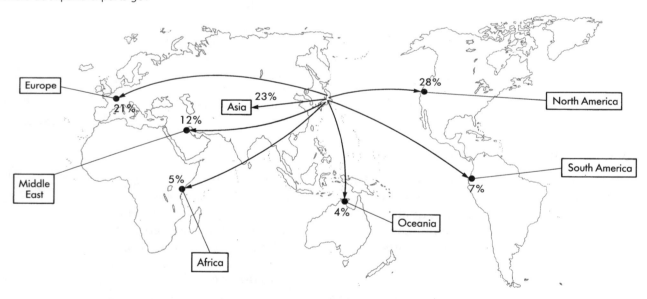

Goods exported include: cars; iron and steel; metals; radios; tape recorders; televisions; optical instruments; motor cycles; transistors; plastics; synthetic fibres; machinery; calculators.

Now test yourself

21 What is meant by the following terms:
imports; exports; balance of trade; manufactured goods?

22 Look at the table on page 43. Which products does Japan import more of than export?

23 (a) Look at the two maps on page 44. Name one area of the world that Japan imports more from than it exports to.
(b) Why do you think the percentage of imports from the area identified in (a) is so high?

24 Use the figures in the table below to draw a divided bar graph.

Goods	Percentage exported	Percentage used for home market
Washing machines	32	68
Microwaves	78	22
Pianos	29	71
Bicycles	13	87
Watches	83	17
Cameras	82	18
Calculators	76	24
Colour TVs	60	40
Refrigerators	25	75
Motor cycles	46	54
Batteries	29	71
Video recorders	82	18

25 Suggest two reasons why international trade is necessary.

Japan in the modern world

Japan is most noted for its technological and industrial strength. Its strong economy makes Japan a very influential trading partner. Most westerners know little about Japanese culture other than sushi, martial arts, and karaoke. But Japan has a rich culture spanning many centuries.

CHAPTER 5

Places in the developing world

CASE STUDY: BANGLADESH

Bangladesh is a very flat, low-lying country formed at the mouth of the great rivers Ganges, Brahmaputra and Meghna.

Bangladesh is one of the poorest countries in the world, with most people living well below the poverty line.

Most of the people in Bangladesh live in the countryside – only 16 per cent live in towns.

The land is very fertile. Annual flooding spreads rich river mud over the plains.

Most people are farmers. They have to grow their own rice to feed their families.

The climate is hot all year round, with a wet season between June and September.

Bangladesh has a population density of about 390 per sq km.

Facts about Bangladesh

Total population	116 million
Area	144 000 sq km
Rates of population growth	2.6% per year
Percentage of population in urban areas	15.7%
Percentage of workers in:	
Primary	61%
Secondary	8%
Tertiary	31%
Life expectancy	51 years
Percentage of population under 15 years	45%
Average income per person	US $130 per year
Percentage of population able to read and write	29%
Population ratio per doctor	10 925

Now test yourself

1 Find a map of south-east Asia in an atlas.
   (a) Name the countries surrounding Bangladesh marked ①–⑤ on the map.
   (b) Name the sea area marked A.
   (c) Name the line of latitude marked with a broken line.

2 Look at the information table on page 46. Bangladesh has a high proportion of its population aged under 15. What problems do you think this could bring?

3 Give two reasons why most people in Bangladesh are farmers.

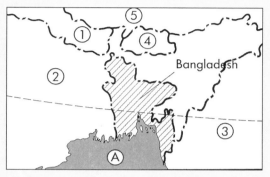

What is it like to live in Bangladesh?

A Bangladeshi woman selling fruit at the local market.

Most people in Bangladesh live in rural areas. They are mainly farmers and live in small village communities.

A Bangladeshi man building a house for himself.

Their houses are huts made out of whatever building materials are available, for example, clay, branches or corrugated tin.

Life in the villages is very basic. There are no sanitation facilities and water is usually obtained from a village pump or well or from the local river or stream. Only a few places have electricity.

A tube well

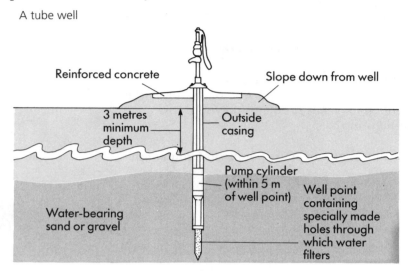

There are few schools. The children lucky enough to have a place in a school often face a long walk each day to get there.

Bangladeshi children playing in the river mud.

Now test yourself

4   Study the three photographs. What do they tell you about life in Bangladesh?

5   Imagine we had photographs of similar activities, but this time taken in Britain. What differences would you expect to see?

A day in the life of a Bangladeshi family

Family: Father aged 34
Mother aged 30
Children aged 14, 12,
10, 8, 6

Morning: The mother gets up, washes, dresses and prepares breakfast for her husband and children, from the curry leftover from the night before. After breakfast the father goes with the two eldest children to their fields which have to be prepared before planting the next rice crop.

The mother keeps the youngest child with her and sends the other two to the village well to fetch some water. (The nearest school is four kilometres away, but there are no places for the children so they help their parents.)

When the children return they have to go to the village laundry – a stream which runs past the village – to do the washing.

Lunchtime: The mother prepares a meal of chappatis and vegetables. One of the children takes some food out to the fields for the others.

Afternoon: The mother leaves the youngest child with an elderly neighbour and takes the other two children to gather firewood. They have to walk several kilometres carrying heavy bundles of sticks.

Evening: The father and two eldest children return from the fields. The oxen are fed and watered. The mother prepares the evening meal of rice and some curry. After the meal is cleared away it has begun to get dark. The family cannot afford oil lamps, so it is time for bed.

Hazards Bangladesh could do without

Bangladesh is a country that has always suffered from flooding. The country itself owes its existence to the rivers depositing huge amounts of silt. This silt gradually builds up, forming a flat plain just above sea level. Much of Bangladesh is less than 15m above sea level.

The 1991 floods in Bangladesh

Many millions of people live in these low-lying lands, as the regular flooding and fertile soils form ideal conditions for rice to grow.

Flooding can come from the rivers or the sea. During springtime, snow melting in the mountains can cause river levels to rise and the risk of flooding to increase. By far the most destructive and life-threatening floods come from the sea. Violent storms called typhoons form out over the Indian Ocean (usually during the autumn).

Occasionally these storms head straight towards Bangladesh. Sea water is driven northwards by the strong winds and funnels into the Bay of Bengal. The extra amount of water and huge waves can easily wash over the low-lying land. Many people may die because they do not have radios or televisions to warn them that a storm is coming.

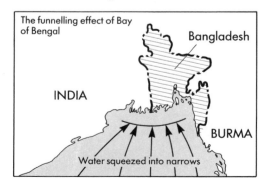

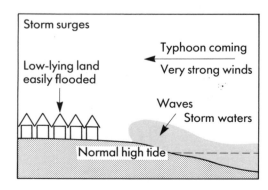

Now test yourself

Read all the information opposite.

10 Why is regular flooding by rivers beneficial to Bangladesh?

11 What is a typhoon?

12 Explain why the shape of the Bay of Bengal increases the effects of typhoons.

13 Every time a typhoon hits Bangladesh thousands die. Give three reasons why the loss of life is always so great.

Bangladesh in the modern world

Bangladesh is not noted as a major strength in world affairs. It is a poor developing country that suffers from major flooding, which causes millions of pounds worth of damage and the loss of many lives. Its economy is based on agriculture and Bangladesh is a net receiver of aid from various world charities. According to the 1993 figures, Bangladeshis were the third poorest of all the nations in the world.

CASE STUDY: BRAZIL

Facts, figures and distribution of population

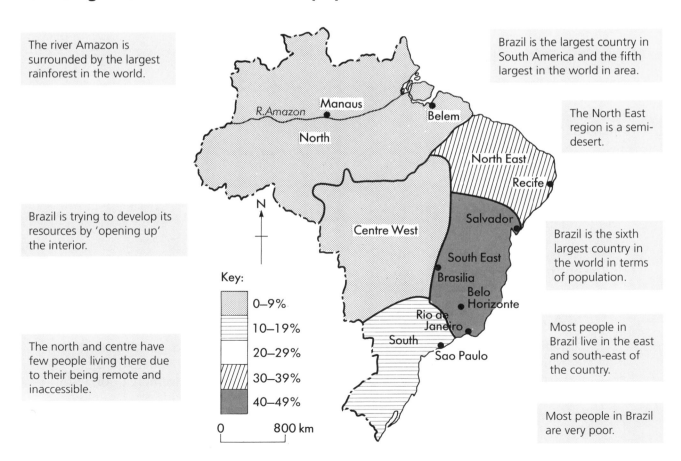

The river Amazon is surrounded by the largest rainforest in the world.

Brazil is the largest country in South America and the fifth largest in the world in area.

The North East region is a semi-desert.

Brazil is trying to develop its resources by 'opening up' the interior.

Brazil is the sixth largest country in the world in terms of population.

The north and centre have few people living there due to their being remote and inaccessible.

Most people in Brazil live in the east and south-east of the country.

Most people in Brazil are very poor.

Key:
- 0–9%
- 10–19%
- 20–29%
- 30–39%
- 40–49%

0   800 km

Facts about Brazil

Total population	158 million	Percentage of population under 15 years	36.3%
Area	8 511 965 sq km	Average income per person	US $2051 per year
Rate of population growth	2.37% per year	Percentage of population able to read and write	76%
Percentage of population in urban areas	70.8%	Population ratio per doctor	2402
Percentage of workers in:			
Primary activities	11%		
Secondary activities	39%		
Tertiary activities	50%		
Life expectancy	Male 62 years; Female 67 years		

Now test yourself

Find a map of South America in an atlas to help you answer these questions, and fill in the map shown above.

14 (a) Name the countries surrounding Brazil marked ①–⑩ on the map.
(b) Name the sea areas marked Ⓐ and Ⓑ.
(c) Name the two lines of latitude marked Ⓒ and Ⓓ.

15 Look at all the information on the table above. Brazil has a high proportion of its population aged under 15. What problems do you think this could bring?

16 Why are there very few people living in the north of Brazil?

A country of contrasts

Differences in wealth exist not only between countries of the world, but are also found within countries. Some parts of Brazil are very wealthy, with all the attractions of a modern society. However, other parts are extremely poor, with many people living in the worst poverty imaginable.

This table shows the contrasts in population and wealth between different regions in Brazil:

Region	Population (% of total)	Share of income (% of total)
North	4	2
Centre West	6	3.1
South	18.1	18.3
South East	42.2	62.8
North East	29.7	13.8

South East Brazil

Copacabana beach in Rio

Carnival time in Rio

South East Brazil has over two third's of the country's income. The reason why South East Brazil is wealthy is because:

- most of Brazil's industry is concentrated here;
- coffee is an important Brazilian export and many wealthy coffee plantations are found in this region;
- it has the natural energy resource of HEP;
- roads and railways in this area are well-developed.

North East Brazil

North East Brazil has many problems:

- low incomes;
- high unemployment;
- very poor living conditions in villages and towns.

Living on the edge of Recife

The reason why there is so much poverty is that:

- there is a lack of rich farm resources and valuable minerals;
- occasional droughts affect the crop production;
- a small number of wealthy families and companies own the land;
- there is a lack of investment in the area by the government and foreign companies.

Now test yourself

Two Brazilians were asked to describe their lifestyles.

17 Using the words below, copy and complete the two paragraphs.
'This is a _____ climate to live in, the sun always shines. My father is a wealthy _____ . He made his money from the profits of his _____ plantation. I have an important job within our company. I am responsible for _____ . I spend lots of time going to _____ and eating out – life can be so hectic sometimes. It's great when the Mardi Gras comes around, I get _____ for a whole week. I love being Brazilian.'

'Life is okay sometimes but most of the time it is one big _____ . My father does _____ to provide me and my six brothers with enough food. We live in a comfortable _____ although it does get a little dirty and _____ sometimes. My job is to fetch the clean _____ everyday. I hope one day to be able to move to the big city and have a _____ job. I think I could be very good at washing cars.'

*shack   parties   proper   superb   his best   struggle   coffee   exports   overcrowded
water   drunk   businessman*

18 Where does the rich Brazilian live?

19 From these paragraphs what can you tell about the lifestyle of the people involved?

20 How do the two paragraphs together reflect modern Brazil?

The rainforest

Much of northern Brazil has very few people living in it because it is part of the huge Amazon rainforest. It is a source of great wealth, for many different reasons:

- the trees provide valuable timber, much in demand for furniture making;
- the leaves, bark and roots of many of the forest plants provide us with important medicines;
- the rainforest itself is home to many different species of plants, animals, birds and insects;
- the vast numbers of trees produce much of the oxygen in the air.

The Amazon rainforest

Equator

N

0   1000km

Dense vegetation encroaching into one of the many rivers at the Amazon basin

The native inhabitants of the Amazon rainforest are tribal Indians. It is not known for certain when the Indians first settled in the forests, nor where they came from, but it is thought that they have been living their traditional way of life for thousands of years. Their way of life was very simple. The forest provided all their building materials, medicines and weapons. Their food came from a variety of sources, they **hunted** for meat and skins; **gathered** fruits, berries, nuts and edible plants; **fished** in the many rivers; and **farmed** using simple 'slash and burn' agriculture.

Preparing poisoned darts

An Indian settlement

'Slash and burn' involved cutting down and burning a small area of forest, the ashes being used as a fertiliser. (Rainforest soils are very poor and useless for full-scale crop growing.) After a couple of years the soil would lose its nourishment, and so the tribe of Indians would move on to another patch of forest. The abandoned clearing was soon overgrown by the forest again. Hunting in a different area would also allow the old area to recover its population of animals. Using the forest in this way did no permanent damage.

Now test yourself

21 Look at the drawing on page 56, which shows a typical Amazonian Indian scene.

Match each of the following statements with their correct number:

(a) hunting in the forest; (b) fishing nets hanging out to dry; (c) a dug out canoe; (d) wood cut for fuel; (e) communal hut for sleeping; (f) crops growing in the 'garden'; (g) cooking using clay pots; (h) a hammock for sleeping; (i) food already gathered.

22 Name four items shown in the diagram made of wood, and three made of grasses or reeds.

Changes that affected the Indians

Brazil is a very large country, with a large population which is growing rapidly. The cities were becoming so overcrowded and Brazil was becoming so poor that during the mid 1960s, the Brazilian government took the decision to open up the rainforest areas.

The trans-Amazonian highway

Opencast mining

Their aim was to:

- develop the vast resources that lay within and beneath the Amazonian area;
- develop new industry which would create wealth for Brazil;
- create more land for settlement, where people could farm their own land and so move out of the crowded cities.

Vast areas of rainforest were cut down as new roads and towns were built; new farms were created; and areas of opencast mining were developed.

Cutting down the rainforest has created many problems

Valuable timber is simply being burned, which increases the carbon dioxide levels of the atmosphere. This could affect the world's climate.

Many plants, animals and insect species will be wiped out and lost forever.

Soils are very poor, so growing crops is unsuccessful.

Much of the land is now given over to grazing cattle for American hamburgers.

Indian tribes are losing their land, their culture and their hunting grounds. Their traditional way of life is being lost forever. They are being forced into cities, where they live in desperate poverty.

Much of the soil is washed into rivers, which are silting up and flooding more frequently.

Remember: once the rainforest has been destroyed it will never grow again – it is lost FOREVER.

Now test yourself

Changes in the Amazon rainforest

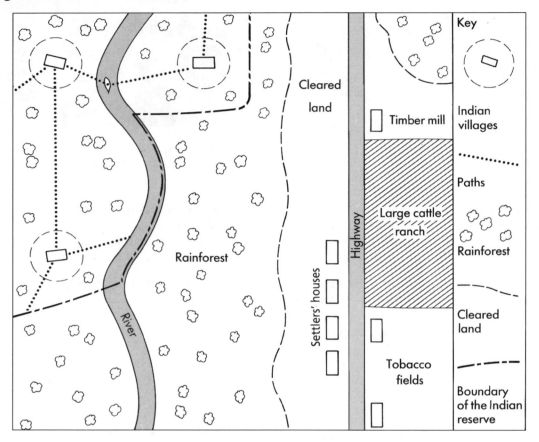

23 What was this area like before settlers moved in?

24 Describe the main changes that have taken place.

25 How has it been possible for settlers to clear large areas of rainforest?

26 Why are the settlers' houses built near the highway?

27 How do the settlers make a living in the forest?

28 How would you feel about the changes if you were:
   (a) an Indian living in this area?
   (b) the owner of the large cattle ranch, who lives in the USA?
   (c) the wife of a poor settler who works in the timber mill?

29 Do you think it is good that a reserve has been created for the Indians?

CHAPTER 6

*T*he active Earth

T HE EARTH'S CRUST

The Earth's crust is made of a series of ridged **plates** that fit together like pieces of a jigsaw. These plates float on the molten interior of the Earth and so move independently of each other. It is where one plate comes into contact with another that many of the world's major earthquakes and volcanoes can be found. The plate boundaries are where we find the 'active' areas of the world. The study of the movement of these plates is called **plate tectonics**.

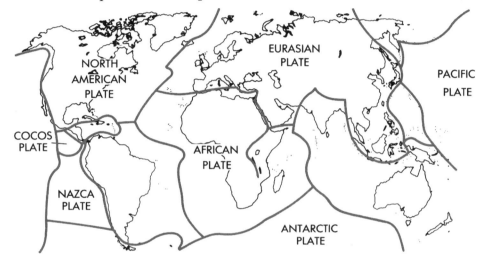

The plate boundaries

Now test yourself

Major earthquakes				Major volcanoes	
Year	**Location**	**Intensity**			
1920	Southern China	8.6		Mount St. Helen's	USA
1968	Japan	8.6		Mount Shasta	USA
1964	Alaska	8.5		Aconcagua	Argentina
1962	Chile	8.5		Paricutin	Mexico
1927	S E China	8.3		Mauno Loa	Hawaii
1923	Japan	8.3		Popocatapeti	Mexico
1906	San Francisco	8.3		Surtsey	Iceland
1976	S China	8.0		Vesuvius	Italy
1985	Mexico	7.8		Etna	Italy
1995	Kobe, Japan	7.5		Cotopaxi	Ecuador
1987	Armenia	7.5		Stromboli	Italy
1985	Chile	7.4		Tristan de Cunha	South Atlantic
1968	Iran	7.4		Kilimanjaro	Tanzania
1991	Southern California	7.3		Fuji Yama	Japan
1980	Italy	7.2		Krakatoa	Indonesia
1988	San Francisco	6.9			
1963	Yugoslavia	6.0			

1   Use an atlas and a blank physical map of the world to:
    (a) mark the plate boundaries.
    (b) mark each major earthquake with a blue dot.
    (c) mark each major volcano with a red dot.

2   What do you notice about the distribution of most of the major earthquakes and volcanoes? How do you account for this?

3   Why do you think there are no major volcanoes or earthquakes in Britain at the present time?

Earthquakes

Every now and again we hear on the news that an earthquake has caused widespread damage and death somewhere in the world. These events are timely reminders of the destructive powers of the planet on which we live. Earthquakes are very common, although most of them are so small that they can only be detected by sensitive scientific instruments. Earthquakes only become news when major centres of population are affected.

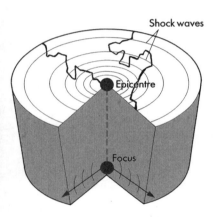

Earthquake damage in Alaska

An earthquake is a series of shock waves passing through the rocks of the Earth's crust. Most last for less than a minute, but in that time the shaking ground causes many buildings to collapse, roads and railways to crack, and gas and water mains to fracture. They may even lead to huge tidal waves called **tsunamis**. It is falling masonry, flying glass and fire which kill many people during and after an earthquake.

The Richter Scale	
<3.5	Only recorded by sensitive instruments
3.5–4.8	Feels like a lorry passing
4.9–5.4	Loose things fall
5.5–6.1	Walls crack
6.2–6.9	Chimneys fall, some buildings collapse
7.0–7.3	Many buildings fall, landslides
7.4–8.1	Most buildings and bridges destroyed
>8.1	Total destruction

A seismograph

Earthquakes occur deep within the Earth where the pressure that has built up in the crust is suddenly released. The exact place where it occurs is called the **focus**. The point on the surface immediately above the focus is called the **epicentre**. The magnitude or intensity of an earthquake is measured on the Richter Scale and recorded on a seismograph.

Case study: Earthquake in Mexico

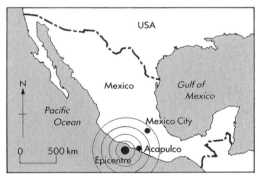

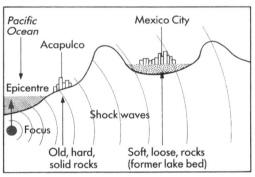

At 8.43 am on September 19th 1985, just as the morning rush hour was coming to a close, an earthquake measuring 7.8 on the Richter scale struck the 18 million inhabitants of Mexico City.

Schools, apartments, office blocks, churches and hotels came crashing down. Fires broke out as gas mains exploded. First pictures suggested that about one-third of the city had been devastated. President Miguel de la Madrid declared the city a disaster area and appealed for international help.

Rescue work went on in appalling conditions. They had to work quickly to free the thousands of business people, families and tourists trapped under the rubble. There was no light, no water and only limited amounts of petrol. Police feared that further tremors would cause more buildings to collapse. Communications were non-existent and many streets were blocked with debris. It was impossible to tell how many people had died.

Hospitals still able to operate were working on full emergency, although blood for the injured was running out and the government appealed for donors.

Now test yourself

Read the passage carefully and look at the photographs and diagrams on the previous page before answering the questions.

5   Why was the timing of the earthquake important?

6   What problems were caused by the earthquake?

7   What problems did rescue workers face?

8   Why was it impossible to tell how many had died?

9   Approximately how far was Mexico City from the epicentre?

10 Acapulco was much closer to the epicentre than Mexico City, yet it suffered less damage. Look at the diagrams carefully and suggest a reason for this.

CHAPTER 7

Shaping the land

W EATHERING

All surfaces that are exposed to the weather are attacked by weathering. Metal rusts, roads crack, statues crumble, and rocks and buildings break up. Evidence of the effect of the weather can be seen all around.

Chemical weathering

Types of weathering

There are three types of weathering.

Physical weathering

This is where rocks are broken down into smaller and smaller particles. One way in which this happens is through freeze/thaw action. Water that has collected in cracks and hollows in the rock will freeze when temperatures fall below 0°C. As it does so it expands, increasing pressure on the rock. When it thaws the pressure is released. Repeated freezing and thawing causes the rock to weaken and crumble, so eventually the crack becomes wider. Whole blocks of rock can break off in this way. Freeze/thaw action is commonest in mountain areas where temperatures fluctuate around 0°C for much of the year.

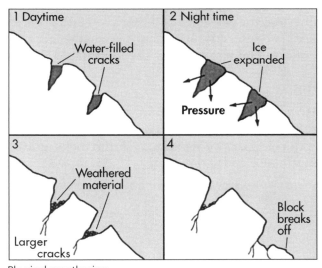

Physical weathering

Large sharp-edged rocks build up at the bottom of slopes

Chemical weathering

As rainwater falls through the air it becomes a very weak type of acid. When this acidic water comes into contact with rock it starts to dissolve it. The rate at which it dissolves depends on the type of rock. Limestone, for example, dissolves very quickly. Many buildings are built partly of limestone and the results of chemical weathering can clearly be seen. Oxygen in the air can sometimes react with iron in the rocks so that they change to a deep red colour – the rocks actually become 'rusty'.

Pollution in towns and cities also increases chemical weathering. Evidence for this can be seen on blackened buildings.

A rock stained by chemical weathering

Just like physical weathering, the presence of water is essential for chemical weathering to take place. The rate at which chemical weathering takes place depends on the temperature. The warmer it is, the more rapid the chemical decay.

Biological weathering

Animals and plants also cause weathering. Seeds may fall into cracks in the rocks. As water usually collects there, it forms ideal conditions for the seed to germinate and grow. As the plant develops, its roots may push the rocks apart. Animals burrowing into the soil can also cause damage.

Now test yourself

Fieldwork/enquiry

1   Visit a cemetery (make sure you ask an adult's permission before entering). Gravestones can be made of different kinds of rock. Rocks can usually be recognised by their colour. Common graveyard rocks include marble (white), limestone (grey) and granite (pink or black). The date on each gravestone gives an idea of how long that piece of rock has been open to the weather. Compare the amount of decay on (a) two gravestones of similar age but different rock types, and (b) two gravestones of the same rock but of different age.

Describe how the amount of weather is affected by rock type and time.

EROSION TRANSPORTATION AND DEPOSITION

The difference between weathering and erosion is that weathering rots the rocks and erosion removes them. Weathering prepares the rock for erosion. After rocks have been affected by weathering they are then prone to erosion.

Erosion occurs where particles of rock or soil are:

*   washed away by a river;
*   removed by waves in the sea;
*   crushed under a glacier;
*   blown away by the wind.

Erosion occurs where nature is very powerful or is said to possess a lot of energy. This could be where:

*   a river flows very fast;
*   large waves are whipped up by a storm and crash onto the coastline;
*   thick ice presses down on the Earth's surface;
*   the wind is strong enough to pick up particles of rock.

Transportation occurs when the material has been 'picked up' and moved to another place. The distance covered may be small (for example, from the front of a beach to the back of the beach) or large (for example, hundreds or even thousands of miles down a river).

Deposition occurs when the transported materials are eventually deposited or dumped. Deposition occurs where:

*   a river flows slowly;
*   the sea washes up gently against a beach;
*   the ice of a glacier begins to melt;
*   areas are sheltered from the wind.

THE RIVER STORY

Much of the water that falls from the sky as precipitation ends up in a river. All rivers begin their lives as small trickles somewhere up in the hills. The start of a river is called its **source**. As it starts to move downhill it creates for itself a narrow **channel** along which it flows. The edges of the channel are marked by the river's banks. Near its source the river channel is narrow, but as it moves downstream more water flows into the river, so the channel gets wider. Two rivers may join together. A small river flowing into a larger river is called a **tributary**. Eventually each river ends at its **mouth**, that is, where it reaches the sea.

The Exe near its source

The Exe at Tavistock

Exmouth

Now test yourself

Look at the sketch map of the River Exe. Find a map of Devon in an atlas.

2 Name area A, the highland where the source of the Exe is found.

3 Name the towns marked B and C. Which town is closer to the mouth?

4 Name the tributary marked D.

5 Name the sea area E into which the river Exe flows.

6 In which direction does the Exe flow?

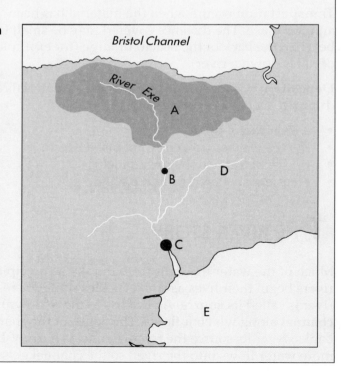

How rivers shape the land

All rivers flow from mountains to the sea and as they do so they have the ability to shape the land. Rivers use **energy** to erode, transport and deposit material. The amount of energy a river has depends on the steepness of the land over which it is flowing (because water always flows downhill, due to gravity) and how much water is in the river. Generally the steeper the land and the more water in the channel, the faster the river flows. When a river has a lot of energy (i.e. when it is flowing quickly, or after heavy rain) it has the ability to erode its bed and banks, and can transport eroded material more easily. When a river loses energy, it no longer has the ability to transport its materials so deposition occurs. The amount of erosion varies considerably from day to day and season to season. Remember that rivers are 'lazy' – they find the easiest possible way to the sea.

A river erodes through:

- **corrasion** where the material carried along within the river crashes into the bed and banks, causing material to break off;
- **attrition** where the particles knock together whilst being carried along by the river;
- **abrasion** which is a common name used to describe both corrasion and attrition;
- **corrosion** where the river water dissolves some or all of the rocks over which it flows;
- **hydraulic action** where the air trapped in cracks and holes is compressed, which leads to the weakening of material along the bed and banks of the river;
- **cavitation** which occurs mainly in waterfalls, where millions of bursting bubbles send out shock waves that weaken the rocks.

A river transports material through:

- **suspension** by carrying small particles along within the river, the amount of suspended material that can be carried depends on the speed of the river (after heavy rain many rivers turn brown with sediment);
- **solution** by dissolving materials resulting from corrosion;
- **traction** by rolling larger rocks and pebbles which cannot be lifted along the bed of the river;
- **saltation** by particles jumping downstream.

Deposition occurs when a river starts losing its energy. Heavier particles get deposited first. The lighter material is transported as long as the river has enough energy. Eventually, much of the lighter material is dumped, although sometimes not until the river reaches its mouth. The river therefore sorts out material as it deposits.

Now test yourself

Look carefully at the photograph. It shows that erosion, transportation and deposition can occur side by side in a river.

7   How does X show evidence of deposition?

8   How does Y show evidence of transportation?

9   How does Z show evidence of erosion?

Shapes created by rivers

As a river moves down its valley its character changes, and so too do the landforms which it creates.

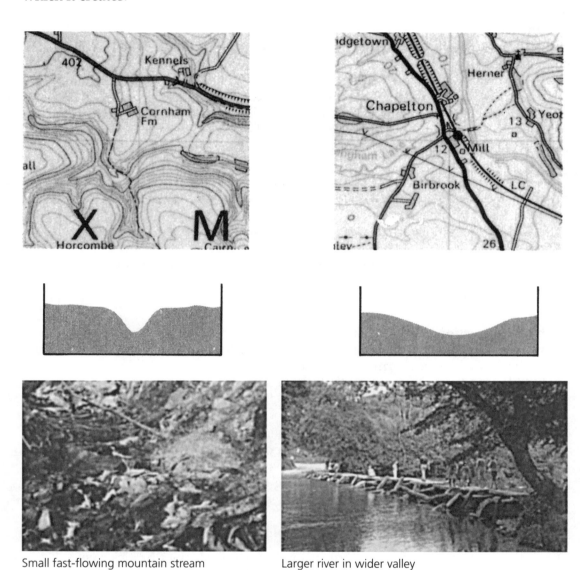

Small fast-flowing mountain stream

Larger river in wider valley

The upper course of a river

In the upper course, a river is usually small but flows very fast. Energy levels are high and the river cuts away at its bed. As it does so, it quickly deepens its valley through 'downcutting', which creates a steep-sided V-shaped valley. Erosion is the dominant process. Several characteristic landforms are found in the upper course.

Waterfalls and gorges

One way in which a waterfall can occur is when hard rock lies over the top of softer rock. The softer rock is eroded more easily, which leaves the harder rock overhanging. Eventually, after undercutting has occurred, the harder rock collapses into the river. The waterfall retreats to a position further upstream. If this process happens several times then a steep-sided gorge is left downstream of the waterfall. This can be seen clearly at High Force waterfall on the River Tees (opposite).

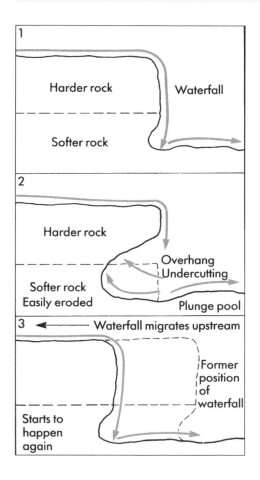

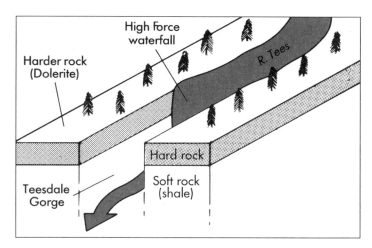

Interlocking spurs

As the river starts to wind its way down its valley it creates a series of **interlocking spurs**. These are small hills that fit together neatly like the pieces of a jigsaw, around which the river flows.

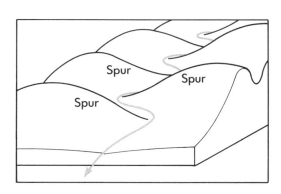

Interlocking spurs

The middle course of a river

As a river moves down its valley a number of changes occur:

* the river gets wider as more and more tributaries join together;
* the valley sides become less steep, giving a much more open V-shape;
* instead of the river eroding downwards into its bed, it begins to erode sideways into its banks, which opens out the valley floor and a flood plain starts to develop;
* erosion still occurs but there is also some deposition;
* the edges of the flood plain are marked by bluffs.

Meanders

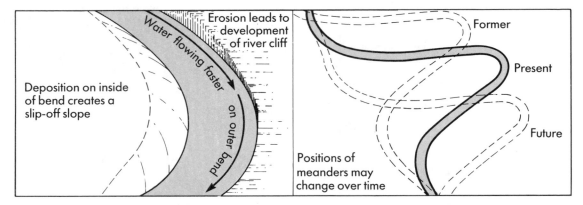

Deposition on inside of bend creates a slip-off slope

Water flowing faster on outer bend

Erosion leads to development of river cliff

Former

Present

Future

Positions of meanders may change over time

A river seldom flows in a straight line. As it wanders from side to side it creates loops, called meanders. Water travels faster on the outside of bends so the river erodes its banks, while on the inside of the bends deposition occurs in the slacker water.

Meanders are constantly changing and over time can actually move downstream.

A cross-section of a meander

Deposition

Undercutting on outer bend

Flood plains

A flood plain is a flat area of land found on the floor of the valley, immediately next to a river. This is the area that is affected by flood waters after excessively heavy rain. It is formed by the river meandering from side to side, wearing away the valley's spurs. Flood plains are covered with layers of **alluvium** (the fine, muddy material spread by a river during floods).

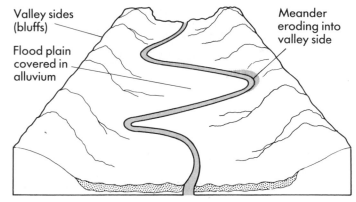

Valley sides (bluffs)

Flood plain covered in alluvium

Meander eroding into valley side

The lower course of a river

As a river approaches its mouth, more subtle changes occur in its character. The valley's V-shape is now so wide that the valley sides have all but disappeared. The river now winds its way slowly across a large flood plain. Deposition is now the dominant process.

In Britain most rivers are not long enough or large enough to develop the full-scale features found in the lower courses of many of the world's great rivers, such as the Mississippi. Instead, many British rivers end their journeys to the sea in an estuary.

T OO MUCH WATER!

Sometimes a river can carry so much water that it cannot all be contained in the river's channel. As more water is added, the river 'bursts its banks' and floods the surrounding countryside. Most floods occur after a period of heavy rain when the amount of water entering the river is more than it can cope with. If rainwater reaches the river quickly then this could lead to an increased risk of flooding. The concrete and tarmac of towns and cities do not allow water to soak into the ground. Instead it runs into drains, which may ultimately empty into a river. So, more water reaches the river in less time. This could cause a flood.

Flooding of the River Severn

When a river 'bursts its banks' the effect on the surrounding countryside can be devastating. The flood waters carry mud, stones and various items that have been washed away. When this water and mud mixture washes into people's homes, it causes damage to personal possessions and the structure of the houses themselves. The water damages cars and anything in its path.

Sometimes small streams become raging torrents which have the power to uproot trees and wash away buildings. Bridges can trap fallen branches and trees, causing water to build up even more – increasing the effect of the flood still further. Farmland can be inundated and livestock threatened or crops destroyed. Roads become impassable and normal everyday life is severely disrupted. In severe floods there is the possibility of loss of life with the increased risk of accidents.

When the flood waters drain away the effects remain. People have to clean up their houses, and repairs have to be made to services (such as roads, railway lines, bridges, drains, etc.) before life can return to normal.

Flooding in the Lower Wye Valley

Flood prevention

Some places are particularly prone to flooding. These high risk areas are sometimes found in the middle of towns. If people and property are regularly affected by flood waters it may become feasible to protect the threatened area. Flood prevention schemes may involve building walls or embankments or even widening or dredging the river. The idea is that the water in the river will be quickly channelled away rather than flowing over its banks into the surrounding town. One such scheme can be found in Monmouth.

Case study: The Monmouth scheme

The river Wye as seen from Monmouth Bridge

Banking along the river Monnow

Monmouth has a long history of flooding. The local school and playing fields have been regularly under water. The town centre itself has been flooded no less than seven times since 1910. Monmouth is particularly prone to flooding due to the fact that the river Monnow joins the river Wye in the town. The commonest pattern of flooding is that the Monnow overflows first, followed between 18 to 36 hours later by the river Wye, thus causing a second flood in the town.

Before the scheme (artist's impression)

Part of the completed flood defence scheme

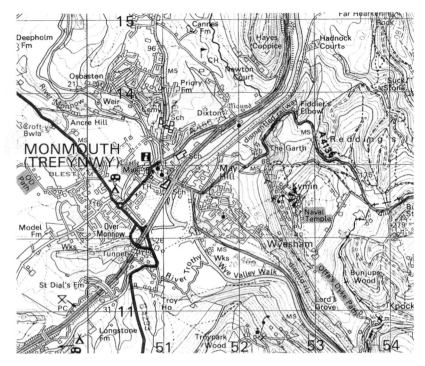

Considerable public anxiety was evident following the flood of 1979. This flood affected at least 190 commercial, industrial and residential properties. After a lengthy feasibility study and public enquiry, the go-ahead was finally given for the £1.15 million scheme in July 1988, the work being completed in the spring of 1990.

The aim was to protect the town from the highest flood expected in one hundred years. The river Monnow had been widened in the 1930s and could not be widened again so the only alternative was the building of walls and embankments. Along the river Wye, a small bank was constructed together with flood gates and flap valves (hinged flaps which open during times of flood to prevent water reaching the town).

Monmouth's historical interest needed to be preserved

One problem that had to be overcome was that in Monmouth the immediate surroundings of the river were of special historical interest.

'The raising of walls and embankments for the flood alleviation scheme necessarily has an impact on the environment. In designing the works, the aim has been to construct defences that are both functional in an engineering sense, and yet sensitive to the environment in which they are built.' (*National Rivers Authority*)

Storm hydrographs

The amount of water in a river is greatly affected by the total amount of rain over a period of time. A storm hydrograph helps us gauge whether a particular river will flood or not. This is a graph showing the amount and intensity of rainfall related to the amount of water flowing in the river (the **discharge**).

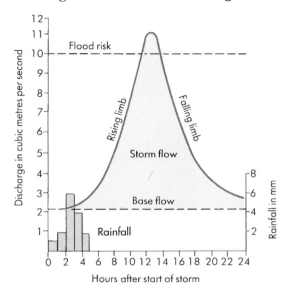

The amount of rainfall is shown as a bar graph and the discharge as a line graph. Notice how the amount of water in the river begins to rise soon after the rain starts. Water takes some time to flow over the land, so the peak discharge comes after the peak rainfall. The time difference between the two is called the **lag**.

Notice how the base flow remains more or less constant. This is the groundwater entering the river. It shows what the river level would have been if it had not rained. Groundwater allows rivers to flow even when it has not rained for several weeks.

The area marked **storm flow** represents the extra amount of water in the river as a result of the storm. The river will only flood when the peak discharge line rises over the flood risk line.

As rain falls the river level will inevitably rise, but the rate at which it rises, and therefore the risk of flooding, depend on a number of factors.

- Very heavy rain for a short period of time is more likely to cause a flood than the same amount of rain over a longer period of time.
- Some rocks do not allow water to soak in (they are **impermeable**) so water runs off the surface and quickly reaches the river. Some rocks soak up a lot of water so it takes a long time for the extra water to reach the river.
- In towns and cities, drains and sewers allow storm waters to reach the river quickly, so that downstream of a town the risk of flooding may be greater.
- Some rivers are very long so that the extra water is spread over a greater length, lessening the risk of flooding. Shorter rivers have less time to adjust to the extra water.
- Sometimes the surface may already be waterlogged. This again means that water will run off and quickly reach the river.

Now test yourself

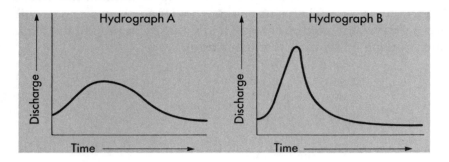

Look carefully at the two hydrographs.

10 Match each of these statements with the correct hydrograph: permeable rock; impermeable rock; urban area; rural area; gentle rising limb; steep rising limb.

11 Which hydrograph suggests the greater flood risk? Explain your answer.

CHAPTER 8

*U*sing water

THE HYDROLOGICAL CYCLE

About two-thirds of the Earth's surface is covered by water, with nearly 97.5% being salt water and only 2.5% being fresh water. By far the greatest amount of water is found in the oceans. Water is transferred from the surface to the air by evaporation, especially in hot climates. Winds blow moist air around until eventually it falls back to the surface as rain, snow or some other form of precipitation. Only about 21% of all precipitation falls over the land and when it does, it can either:

- soak into the soil and rocks and become part of the groundwater;
- remain frozen and become part of an ice sheet or glacier;
- stay on the surface as part of a river or lake;
- be taken up and used by plants;
- or be quickly evaporated back into the air.

All water will eventually end up back in the ocean. It may take a long time (as in the case of an ice sheet), or be very quick (as in the case of rain falling directly into the sea). The **water cycle** (or hydrological cycle) means that over the whole globe the amount of water taken out of the oceans through evaporation is exactly equal to the amount washed in by rivers.

To understand the water cycle it is important that you are familiar with these words:

- **precipitation** is water in its many forms falling from the sky as rain, hail, snow, frost and dew;
- **condensation** is the change from water vapour to liquid water, as air rises in the atmosphere it cools, condensation occurs and clouds form;
- **evaporation** is the change from liquid water to water vapour, this usually happens when the surface of the Earth is warmed;
- **transpiration** is water given off by plants;
- **run off** is water running across the surface of the land, usually as a river;
- **throughflow** is water running underground through the rocks;
- **groundwater** is water stored in the rocks as part of the water table.

Water store	How long the water can remain there
Atmosphere	hours ⟶ weeks
Surface	days ⟶ hundreds of years
Groundwater	one year ⟶ thousands of years
Ice sheets	tens of thousands of years
Oceans	years ⟶ tens of thousands of years

Now test yourself

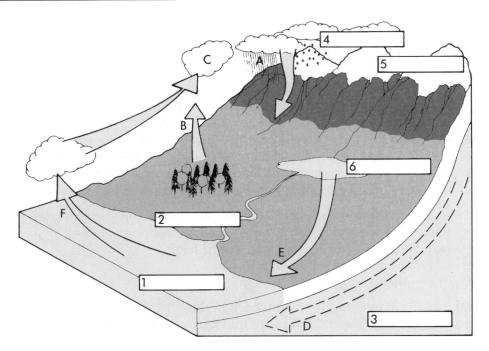

1   The diagram above shows the stores and links within the water cycle.
Each numbered box shows a store and each lettered arrow shows a link.
Match the words with their correct letter or number: groundwater; snow and ice;
atmosphere; plants; throughflow; run off; precipitation; ocean; transpiration; condensation;
evaporation; rivers and lakes.

S OURCES OF FRESH WATER

Water is essential for our modern way of life. Every one of us in Britain uses on
average about 100 litres of clean, fresh water every day. Even more is used for
farming, industry and recreation and the total amount used is increasing all the
time. Changing lifestyles has led to more water being needed in the home, for
things like automatic washing machines, dishwashers and garden sprinklers. To
make one tonne of steel, 250 000 litres of water are needed.

Irrigating farmland

Costs for water uses per hour:	
Toilet flush 1p	Bath 8p
Shower 4p	Washing machine 13p
Dishwasher 6p	Hosepipe 54p
Rainfall is free. The costs come when water has to be stored, transported and cleaned.	

All our water originally falls as rain. Some of that rainwater is then stored in rocks
as groundwater, or in rivers or reservoirs. It is from these that the water is taken,
treated and pumped into our homes and factories.

A pumping station

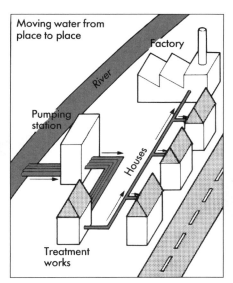

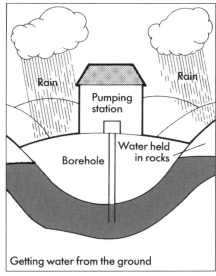

Maintaining supplies

We are very fortunate in this country that it rains quite a lot. This means we have a regular supply of water. But most rain falls in the mountains of the north and west, where demand is low. More water is needed in the south and east, where more people live and where there is more farmland. There is a limit to how much can be taken out of rivers and from the ground, so that means water has to be moved around the country.

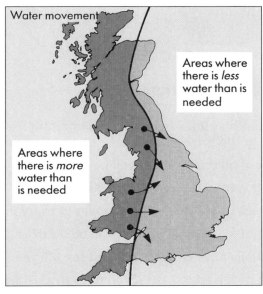

In recent years, water companies have had difficulty in maintaining regular supplies. The problem has been caused by:

- a series of warm, dry summers;
- rain does not always fall where it is most needed;
- in warm weather more water is used – more gardens and parks have to be watered;
- in some areas up to 35% of water is lost through leaks, because water mains are very old;
- increasing demand.

When there is a water shortage it is called a **drought**. If more water is needed, why don't we build more reservoirs?

Should we build a reservoir?

It is proposed to build a dam across the valley of a stream in a highland area. It will create a lake 7 ½ miles square in area, and provide the city 65 miles away (total population 600 000) with a regular supply of fresh water and some electricity. In doing so, it will drown a picturesque village (including 12 houses, a church and a pub) and flood 2500 hectares of valuable farmland.

The valley before the dam is built

How the valley will look after the dam

Now test yourself

2   A scheme such as this often provokes different views from different people. Match each comment to the correct person.

(a) 'Think of all the jobs that will be created.'   Local farmer

(b) 'I don't want to live anywhere else.'   A conservationist

(c) 'We must guarantee water supplies to everyone.'   A watersports enthusiast

(d) 'Think of all the wildlife that will be destroyed.'   Local resident

(e) 'My family have worked this land for 150 years.'   Manager of water company

(f) 'Think of the added attraction to tourists of fishing,   Chairman of 'Damit', the
     sailing and windsurfing.'   construction company

3   Three of the people above are for the scheme and three against. Which are which?

4   Deep, narrow mountain valleys are ideal locations for reservoirs.
    Give three reasons why this is so.

5   The alternative to building more reservoirs is to use water more efficiently.
    Suggest two ways in which we could cut down on the amount of water we use.

D IRTY WATER: EFFECTS AND SOLUTIONS

Many of the pollutants that reach our rivers and seas get there through:

• carelessness;
• lack of concern for our environment;
• because the cost of pollution protection is too high.

Pollution has far-reaching effects, but, given commitment, there *are* solutions to the problem.

Water pollution — the price of progress?

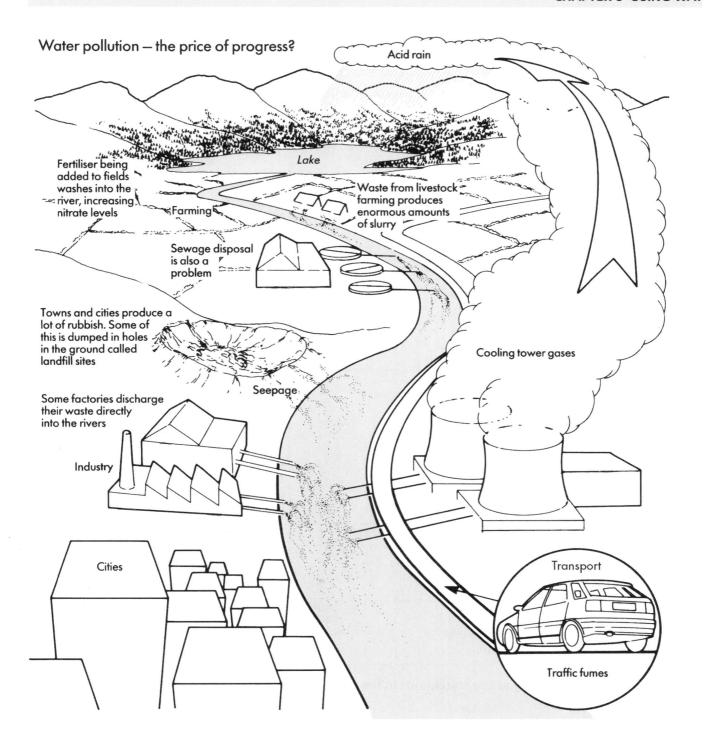

Acid rain

Lake

Fertiliser being added to fields washes into the river, increasing nitrate levels

Farming

Waste from livestock farming produces enormous amounts of slurry

Sewage disposal is also a problem

Towns and cities produce a lot of rubbish. Some of this is dumped in holes in the ground called landfill sites

Seepage

Cooling tower gases

Some factories discharge their waste directly into the rivers

Industry

Cities

Transport

Traffic fumes

Now test yourself

Effects of pollution	Source of pollution	Solutions
Fumes and rainwater mixing together cause acid rain. When it gets into rivers and lakes it kills fish and plants.		Cleaning equipment fitted to cooling towers.
Untreated sewage carries high levels of bacteria which can lead to disease.		Treat sewage more efficiently before it is dumped.
Nitrates in drinking water lead to stomach cancer and are dangerous for pregnant mothers.		Encourage organic farming, using crop rotation and natural fertilisers.
Farmyard waste is very toxic if allowed to reach water courses.		Government investment in recycling factories, extracting reusable fertiliser from farmyard waste.
Rotting domestic rubbish produces dangerous gases. Water seeping through the rubbish washes toxic chemicals into the river.		Encourage people to recycle their household waste, as the city of Sheffield has done.
Uncontrolled discharges from factories can kill aquatic life immediately.		Make individual firms pay heavy fines for pollution incidents or introduce high taxation for major polluters.
Warm water from power stations leads to a reduction in oxygen levels in water, which can kill fish.		Generate electricity using renewable sources of energy.
High concentration of exhaust gases leads to eye irritations and nausea, as well as acid rain.		Fit catalytic converters to all exhausts.

6   Look very carefully at the statements in the table above and the list of different types of pollution below.

Copy out the table, writing the correct source of pollution in the correct box:
factory discharges; landfill seepage; acid rain; traffic fumes; farmyard slurry; nitrates; sewage disposal; power stations.

The North Sea: Europe's dustbin

The North Sea is rapidly becoming one of the most polluted parts of the ocean in the world. This is because the industrial countries which surround it have been dumping industrial waste and toxic chemicals in it for the past 100 years. This shallow sea is now beginning to show signs of the consequences of indiscriminate waste disposal.

The causes of pollution in the North Sea.

Sewage sludge is pumped directly into the sea and so too is waste from industry.

The North Sea has some of the busiest shipping lanes in the world. Oil tankers illegally washing out their tanks cause oil pollution.

Ships dump many industrial waste products, or burn them at sea, hoping they dissolve in the sea water.

Several of Europe's major rivers drain into the North Sea. Each one carries its own cocktail of chemicals as a result of flowing through the industrial heartland of Europe.

Now test yourself

7   Look at the table below. Draw a bar graph to show how much mercury is deposited in the North Sea each year by each river.

8   Use an atlas to name the eight countries which border the North Sea.

River pollution of the North Sea

River	Mercury (tonnes per year)	Cadmium (tonnes per year)	Nitrogen (thousand tonnes per year)	Phosphorus (thousand tonnes per year)
Forth	0.1	2.0	1	–
Tyne	1.4	1.3	1	0.2
Tees	0.6	0.6	2	0.2
Humber	0.7	3.5	41	0.6
Thames	1.1	1.5	31	0.1
Scheldt	1.0	7.4	62	7.0
Rhine	3.9	13.8	420	37.0
Ems	0.4	0.7	22	0.7
Weser	1.1	2.9	87	3.8
Elbe	7.3	8.4	150	12.0

From: The Environment (Collins)

The consequences of pollution in the North Sea

Beaches around the North Sea have become heavily polluted. In 1989 only 22 of Britain's beaches were awarded the coveted EC Blue Flag for cleanliness. Many traditional tourist resorts failed the test.

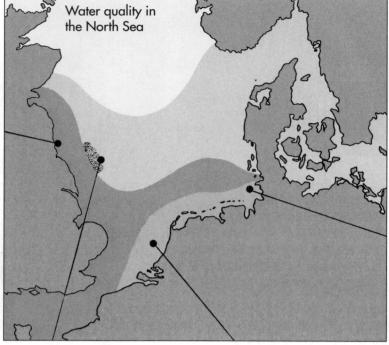

Water quality in the North Sea

Key:

- ☐ Fair
- ☐ Poor
- ■ Very poor
- ■ Extremely poor

Fish stocks are declining. Some of the fish that are caught show the effects of pollution – ulcers, cancerous growths, bulbous eyes, especially in flat fish like plaice which live on the sea bottom. 'Heavy' metals like mercury and cadmium do not dissolve in sea water so they sink to the bottom and build up in the sediment.

Huge blooms of algae have grown, accelerated by the thousands of tonnes of fertiliser washed down rivers.

Marine life is affected. Many seals have died recently as a result of a 'mystery' virus.

Cleaning the North Sea is going to be a very difficult and expensive task. The first task is to get the eight nations to agree on how to do it and who will pay.

Now test yourself

9   You have been asked by your local conservation group to write a letter to your Euro MP. In it you put forward a long-term plan of how to go about cleaning up the North Sea. Make some suggestions about the way the problems can be overcome. You may like to consider:

- How could oil spillage be reduced?
- How could industrial waste dumping be reduced?
- Who will clean up the beaches?
- What about marine wildlife?
- Who will pay for the clean-up?

CHAPTER 9
Weather and climate in Britain

WEATHER MATTERS

The weather affects us all in some way.

Did you need to take a raincoat to school today?

Will it be hot enough to go to the beach at the weekend?

Will there be enough snow to go sledging?

These are some of the many questions we ask when looking at the weather. Some people's jobs are directly affected by the weather, for example, farmers, builders or ice cream vendors.

Extremes of weather may lead to drought or flooding. Strong winds cause storm damage and heavy snow can block roads or even cut off whole villages.

The main feature of the British weather is that it is very changeable. It is the job of the weather forecasters to try and predict what the weather will be like in a few days' time.

MICROCLIMATES

We all know that the weather changes frequently, but not so obvious are the subtle differences that occur in our immediate surroundings. The temperature at any particular place will depend on a number of factors.

- Is it in the shade or direct sunlight?
- Is it sheltered from the breeze or exposed?
- Is it on a surface that reflects or absorbs heat?

Buildings, artificial surfaces and vegetation (or lack of it) affect not only the temperature but also the strength of the wind and the amount of rainfall received. The word **microclimate** is used to describe small-scale changes in the weather.

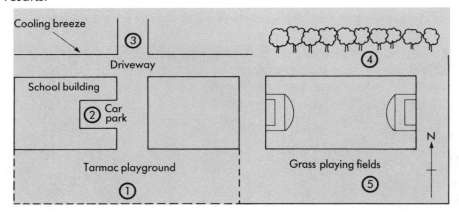

Now test yourself

Fieldwork/enquiry

7   Measure the temperature of at least five sites around your school or garden. Wait for a sunny day and choose your sites carefully. Select a range of positions – some in shade, others in sunshine, some near buildings, others out in the open. Note the wind direction, if any.

Afterwards, look at the data you have collected and account for any differences.

TEMPERATURES ACROSS BRITAIN

Temperatures vary from place to place, from day to day and from season to season. Altitude, latitude and wind direction can all affect how warm or cold it is. The sea also plays a very important role.

Lines on a map joining places of the same average temperatures are called **isotherms**.

July isotherms

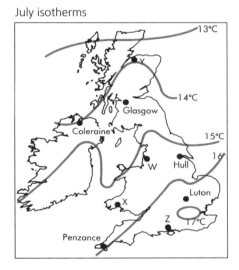

Temperatures during July fall the further north you go. This means that on average, southern England will be warmer than Scotland. In southern Britain the sun is much higher in the sky, so the sun's energy is more intense. The sea is cooler than the land, so coastal areas usually have lower temperatures than places inland. The sea keeps the summer temperatures down.

January isotherms

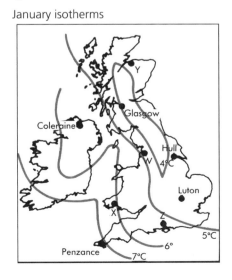

During January, a warm ocean current (the North Atlantic Drift) allows warm air to pass over Britain. Temperatures are kept up so that much of Britain experiences mild winters.

Look at the map on the previous page. Notice how temperatures fall from west to east (i.e. the further away you get from the ocean, the colder the temperature). The sea keeps the winter temperatures up.

Now test yourself

Use both isotherm maps on the previous page to answer these questions:

8   Are these statements true or false?
   (a) Luton has an average July temperature greater than 17°C.
   (b) Penzance has an average January temperature greater than 7°C.
   (c) Glasgow has an average January temperature less than 4°C.
   (d) Both Coleraine and Glasgow are warmer than Hull during July.

9   Use the maps and this table to identify the places marked W, X, Y and Z.

Place	Average July temperature	Average January temperature	Letter
Bournemouth	16–17°C	5–6°C	
Pembroke	15–16°C	6–7°C	
Inverness	13–14°C	3–4°C	
Blackpool	15–16°C	4–5°C	

10 (a) Explain why Coleraine is cooler than Hull during July but warmer than Hull during January.
   (b) Explain why the area to the south of Luton is the warmest part of Britain during July.
   (c) Describe and account for the shape of the 6°C isotherm for January.

R AINFALL ACROSS BRITAIN

The British Isles receives a lot of rain. Usually the air passing over Britain comes from the south-west or west. As it passes over the Atlantic Ocean it picks up moisture through evaporation. By the time it reaches land, the air is wet.

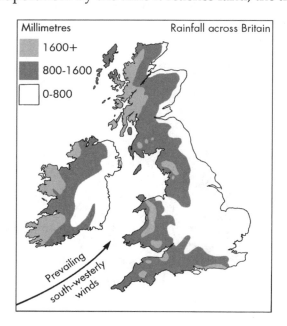

Millimetres — Rainfall across Britain

- 1600+
- 800–1600
- 0–800

Prevailing south-westerly winds

Not everywhere in Britain receives the same amount of rain. As the map shows, western Britain is much wetter than eastern Britain. One reason is because the land is much higher in the west. Generally, the more mountainous the land, the wetter the weather.

Relief rainfall

Rain occurs where air is forced to rise. As it does so, it cools and condensation occurs, so clouds form. In western Britain the air is forced to rise because of the shape of the land. Relief rainfall results.

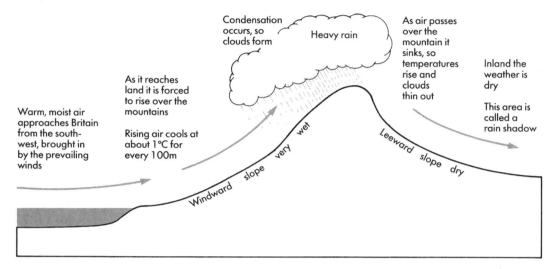

Frontal rainfall

A front occurs where warm air meets cold air. The warm air is forced to rise over the cold air and as it does so, it cools, condenses and forms clouds. Eventually, it will start to rain. Fronts are a very common feature of the British weather. Notice that there is a **warm front** and a **cold front** on the diagram. The warm air of the cold front is forced to rise more steeply and usually brings heavy rain. The clouds are thicker because the air is forced to cool quickly. The warm air at the warm front rises less steeply, so more of the sky is covered with cloud.

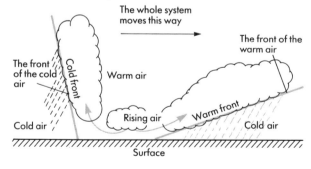

Convectional rain

Convectional rain is associated with very hot, humid weather, so it only rarely occurs in Britain. It happens when the Earth gets so hot that the air immediately above the surface is forced to rise. As it rises it cools, condensation occurs and clouds form. Eventually, very heavy rain falls, often accompanied by thunder and lightning. In some parts of the tropics this type of rain occurs nearly every day, usually during the afternoon.

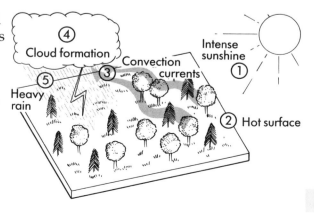

WHAT WILL THE WEATHER BE LIKE TOMORROW?

Forecasting the weather is a very difficult job. Even today, with weather satellites and expensive computers, forecasters get it right only on about seven out of ten occasions. The main reason for this is that the atmosphere is always moving in different directions and it is sometimes difficult to predict which way the air will move.

Pressure gives us a good indication of what the weather will be like for the next few days. Basically, there are two types of pressure.

Air is pressing down on the land surface

This brings fine weather, as clouds do not form

High pressure

Air rises from the land. As it does so, clouds form and eventually it may rain

Low pressure

High pressure: anticyclones

High pressure cells are called anticyclones. They are stable, which means that the same weather may last for a few weeks at a time. An anticyclone during the summer brings fine, hot, sunny weather, but during the winter an anticyclone means fog and very cold temperatures with freezing conditions, but often with clear skies.

Lines joining places of the same pressure are called **isobars**. When isobars are far apart it means gentle winds. If isobars are closely packed together it means strong winds and gales.

High pressure during July

Winter

Summer

High pressure during January

Now test yourself

11 Look at the information on page 90. Can you see two similarities and two differences between an anticyclone in July and an anticyclone in January?

12 What can isobars tell us about the weather?

13 Look at the weather forecast for tomorrow. Are there any 'highs' on the chart? If so, make a note of the forecast. Is the weather forecast the same as you would expect?

Low pressure: depressions

Low pressure cells are called **depressions**. They bring cloud, rain and, in many cases, strong winds. Air spins around the depression and is gradually sucked into the centre where it rises and forms clouds.

In a depression, warm air gets trapped between two areas of colder air. The boundary between the warm and cold air is called a **front**. It is along the front that the heaviest rain occurs.

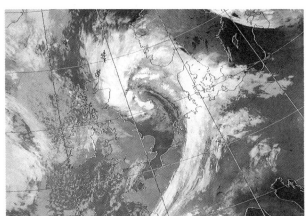
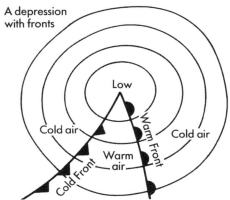

It usually takes two to three days for a depression to pass over the British Isles. During that time the weather can be very changeable, usually following a sequence.

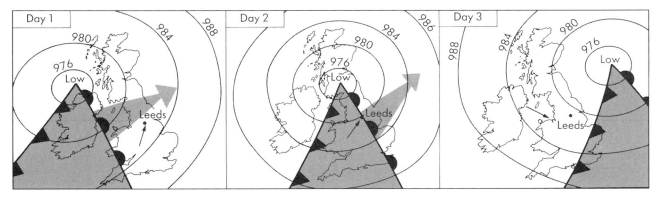

Weather in Leeds as the depression crosses Britain.

Rainfall: none	Rainfall: heavy rain	Rainfall: showers
Wind: from the south	Wind: from the south-west	Wind: from the north-west
Temperature: mild	Temperature: rises	Temperature: drops

Look at the maps on page 91.

14 How do you account for the heavy rain in Leeds on day 2?

15 Why does the temperature change from day to day?

16 Why does the wind keep on changing direction?

THE DIFFERENCE BETWEEN WEATHER AND CLIMATE

The **weather** of an area describes the day to day variations in the atmosphere, whereas the **climate** of a place is the average weather taken over the past 30 years. The climate suggests the sort of weather you may expect.

For example, the climate suggests that Cardiff has an average of 12 rainy days in every December, but the bar graph below shows what actually happened between 1961–90.

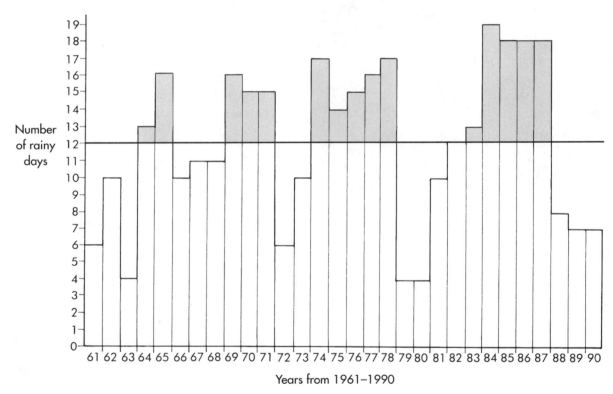

Number of rainy days / Years from 1961–1990

Now test yourself

Look at the figures below, which show the maximum July temperature in Manchester for 1992:

Day	1	2	3	4	5	6	7	8	9	10	11	12	13	14	15	16	17	18	19	20	21	22	23	24	25	26	27	28	29	30	31
°C	17	18	17	14	14	13	13	11	21	20	21	20	21	21	22	22	21	20	19	18	18	20	21	18	15	14	14	14	15	16	16

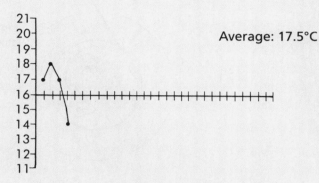

Average: 17.5°C

17 Copy and complete the line graph above using the figures in the table.

18 Shade in red the part of the graph which shows temperatures above average.

19 Shade in blue the part of the graph which shows temperatures below average.

20 Was July 1992 warmer than or cooler than average in Manchester? Justify your answer.

I S BRITAIN'S CLIMATE CHANGING?

The late 1980s and 1990s have seen several dramatic weather events. The years 1987, 1988 and 1990 were three of the warmest years on record, with long periods without rain and sweltering summer temperatures. The years 1987 and 1990 also saw major storms, which caused millions of pounds worth of damage to buildings as well as uprooting millions of trees. Are these the first signs of our changing climate?

The greenhouse effect

Recent scientific evidence has suggested that the whole planet is getting warmer. This may be due to the so called **greenhouse effect**.

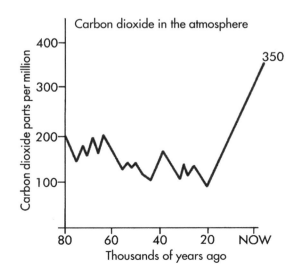

The greenhouse effect is the result of the way we live today. One of the main problems is that too much carbon dioxide is being pumped into the atmosphere. Carbon dioxide controls the heat balance of the earth. It allows heat from the sun in, but does not allow it to escape again. Heat is trapped in the atmosphere, so temperatures rise.

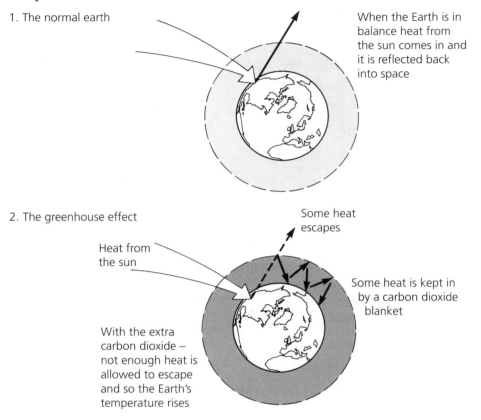

1. The normal earth

When the Earth is in balance heat from the sun comes in and it is reflected back into space

2. The greenhouse effect

Some heat escapes

Heat from the sun

Some heat is kept in by a carbon dioxide blanket

With the extra carbon dioxide – not enough heat is allowed to escape and so the Earth's temperature rises

What causes the problem?

A coal-fired power station

Destroying the rainforest

Carbon is stored in the ground as coal, oil and gas. When we burn these fossil fuels, carbon dioxide is released into the atmosphere.

Trees absorb carbon dioxide, so helping to maintain a balance. Cutting down forests upsets that balance. The problem is increased by burning fallen trees – more carbon dioxide gets into the atmosphere.

What problems will a warmer climate bring?

Nobody really knows what will happen if our world becomes warmer. Some of the effects could be alarming.

What the scientists say

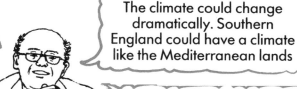

In Britain droughts during the summer and violent storms during the winter could become commonplace

The climate could change dramatically. Southern England could have a climate like the Mediterranean lands

A warmer Earth could cause ice caps and glaciers to melt so sea levels would rise

Areas where a lot of food is grown now could become deserts — where would we grow our food?

Now test yourself

21 These are some of the most populated cities in the world:
London; New York; Calcutta; Mexico City; Tokyo; Djakarta; Cairo; Lagos; Paris; Seoul.
Which of them would be threatened if sea levels rose?
Use an atlas to help you.

22 The map of Britain shows the lowland areas under threat from rising sea levels. Find a map of Britain in your atlas and fit the correct name to each arrow. Choose from this list: Norfolk Broads; Teesside; Severnside; Humberside; Thames Valley; Firth of Forth.

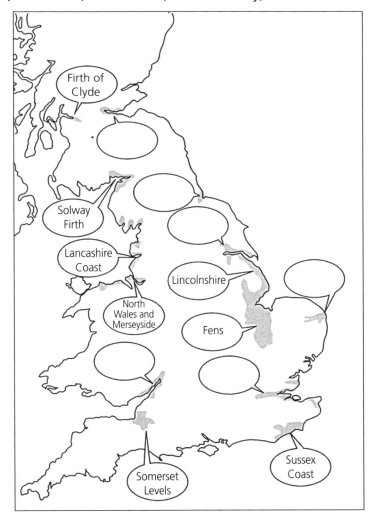

23 List four ways in which individuals can reduce the greenhouse effect.

CHAPTER 10

World climate and vegetation

FACTORS AFFECTING CLIMATE

The climate of an area depends on:

- **nearness to the Equator** because it receives the maximum amount of heat and sunlight and so is generally warmer than elsewhere;
- **height above sea level** because temperatures fall by 6°C per 1000 metre rise, mountains are also wetter than low-lying areas;
- **distance from the sea** because it keeps summer temperatures down and winter temperatures up, coastal areas are also much wetter than inland areas;
- **direction of prevailing winds** if they blow across the sea they bring cloud and rain;
- **ocean currents** because they can raise or lower temperatures considerably, depending on whether they are hot or cold.

The climate plays an important role in determining the type of vegetation found at a particular spot. All plants need sunlight, warmth, nutrients and water in order to survive, so where these are found in abundance, we find a large variety of plants and dense vegetation, e.g. the hot, wet rainforests. Where one of the factors is missing, then only a few specialist plants will be able to survive, so the vegetation cover will be sparse, e.g. the hot deserts.

CASE STUDY: TROPICAL GRASSLANDS

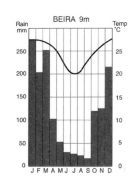

The tropical grasslands, or **savanna** as they are sometimes called, are found between the tropical rainforests and the hot deserts. As the map opposite shows, they rarely extend beyond the tropics. The main areas are the Llanos of Venezuela, the Campos of Brazil, a wide arc-shaped band through central Africa, and in northern Australia.

Savanna landscape during the dry season

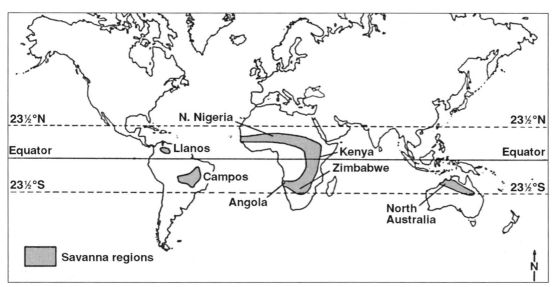

Savanna grassland regions

Bulawayo, Zimbabwe   Latitude of Bulawayo: 20° 10'S. Total rainfall: 589mm

	Jan	Feb	Mar	Apr	May	Jun	Jul	Aug	Sep	Oct	Nov	Dec
Temperature °C	22	23	22	19	16	14	14	15	19	22	23	22
Rainfall (mm)	140	110	82	18	9	2	0	0	4	22	80	122

The main feature of the climate of the tropical grasslands, is that there are two distinct seasons. Both seasons are very hot, but one is wet and the other dry. The rainy, wet season comes during the summer when the overhead sun triggers convectional rain. 95% of all rain can fall in just four months. The dry season is very dry indeed, with severe drought conditions existing for most of the time. These extremes in water availability make life very difficult for plants.

Trees find it difficult to cope with the drought, so only a few are found, such as the baobab tree, scattered across the tropical grasslands. Thorny bushes and shrubs are more common, as their thick outer skins and needle leaves cut down on water loss during the dry season. The main vegetation cover is tall grass. During the wet season the grass is green and lush, but when drought conditions exist it turns into a golden carpet. Fires have always been common due to natural occurrences and human activities, so many trees have thick barks to protect themselves against burning.

Typical savanna vegetation – baobab tree

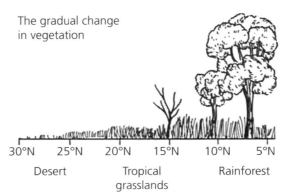

The gradual change in vegetation

Now test yourself

1 Give two ways in which plants in tropical grasslands are adapted to drought conditions.

2 Study the changing vegetation diagram on page 97. Describe what happens to the density of vegetation as latitude changes.

The soils are infertile in tropical grasslands due to all the nutrients being washed down through the soil during the rainy season. In the summer season the soils are baked hard. Under such conditions farming is very difficult.

Human activity

The traditional way of life for savanna peoples is nomadic herding. Tribes wander the plains with cattle or goats. However, this way of life is fast disappearing. In South America much of the land is given over to large-scale cattle ranching. The next time you see a tin of corned beef have a look at the country of origin.

The plains of Africa are the home of the vast herds of animals, such as zebra, wildebeest, giraffe, elephants and the animals that prey on them, such as lions. In parts of East Africa, especially Kenya and Tanzania, tourists are keen to photograph these animals in their natural surroundings. Safari-type holidays are becoming quite popular.

Tourism can be a mixed blessing. Although much needed earnings are brought into the country, it is at the expense of the traditional way of life. Increased numbers of tourists can damage sensitive local environments. Apart from this, much of the money spent on holidays goes to tour operators rather than local people.

One problem facing some parts of the savanna is **desertification**. In recent years the fringes of some grassland areas have become inundated with desert sands. The problem is particularly acute in the Sahel region of Africa. The Sahara desert is advancing southwards. Misuse of the land by overgrazing animals, combined with a long series of dry years, has led to severe drought and soil erosion. In many cases this has led to human tragedy on a vast scale. Horrific scenes of millions dying through starvation created by famine, have been an all too common occurrence on our television screens during the past 10 years.

CHAPTER 11

*P*opulation

D ISTRIBUTION OF POPULATION

At present there are over 5 billion people living on Earth and by the end of the century this will have increased to over 6 billion. Nearly half of all the people that have ever lived are alive today.

However, as the map shows, the world's population is not spread evenly across the globe. In fact, half of all the people occupy only one twentieth of the land surface. Human beings can only live where conditions are right for life, so people are attracted to the most suitable areas. Few live in less favourable regions, as survival would prove difficult for large numbers of people.

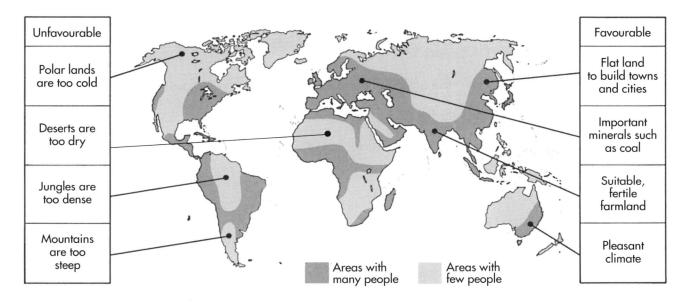

Unfavourable
- Polar lands are too cold
- Deserts are too dry
- Jungles are too dense
- Mountains are too steep

Favourable
- Flat land to build towns and cities
- Important minerals such as coal
- Suitable, fertile farmland
- Pleasant climate

Areas with many people   Areas with few people

The number of people living in an area is called the **population density**. It is worked out by dividing the total population by the total area.

The population density of the UK:

$$\frac{\text{Population}}{\text{Area}} = \frac{57\ 080\ 000}{245\ 000\ \text{square km}} = 233 \text{ people per square km}$$

The UK is quite densely populated, but compare it to Hong Kong which has a population density of 4 073 per square kilometre. Most cities have a much higher density of population than rural areas.

Case study: The population of Egypt

Egypt is a large country in North Africa. It has an area of 1 001 000 square kilometres and a total population of 57 million. Much of the country is desert, except for a narrow strip of land on either side of the River Nile.

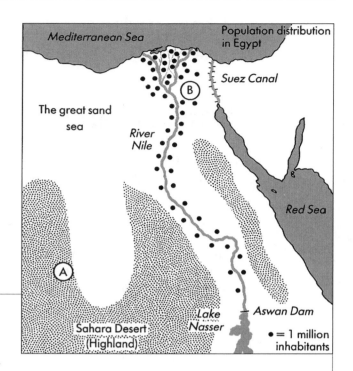

Now test yourself

Look at all the information on Egypt.

1 Work out the population density for Egypt.

2 Describe the distribution of the Egyptian population (how it is spread out).

3 Why is the population density figure misleading?

4 Give two reasons why area A would be unsuitable for large numbers of people.

5 Give two reasons why area B is suitable for inhabitation.

BIRTH AND DEATH RATES AND POPULATION SIZE

By comparing the number of people who are born (birth rates) with the number who die (death rates) for a particular country we can work out whether the population is rising or falling. If more people are born than die (the birth rate is higher than the death rate), then the population will rise. The greater this difference, the faster the population will rise. This rate of natural increase is much higher in developing countries of the world.

Now test yourself

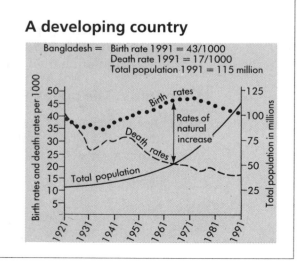

6   Copy and complete the graph for the UK, using the figures below.

	1971	1981	1991
Birth rates	12	13	13
Death rates	10	12	12
Total population	56	56	57

7   Shade the area of the graph showing the 'natural increase'.

8   Look at the graph for Bangladesh.
     (a) In which year were death rates higher than birth rates?
     (b) What would happen to the total population during this time?

9   Compare the two graphs. Identify four differences and two similarities between the two countries.

POPULATION CHANGE

The world's population is growing very rapidly and for the past 100 years or so the Earth has experienced a **population explosion**.

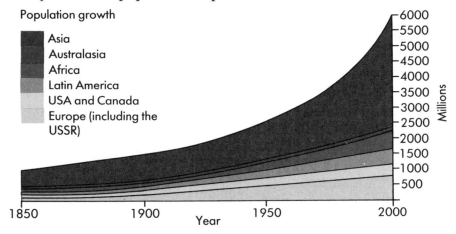

Population growth

Knowing what the total population will be in a few years time is very important. The following points must be carefully estimated when planning for the future:

*   how many houses will be needed?
*   how much food will have to be grown?
*   what about the number of schools?

Not everywhere in the world has had the same rate of change. The most rapid growth in population has occurred in the poorer, developing countries while the richer, developed countries have seen little or no growth. Also, in many countries, millions of people have moved from the countryside into urban areas. As a result of this, the latter part of the century has seen a rapid increase in the number of people living in cities.

The percentage of the world's population living in towns and cities has increased in the last 70 years

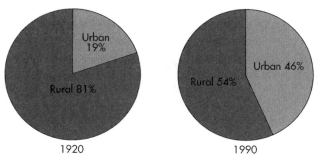

The total population will change when the balance between the number of people being born (the birth rate) and the number of people who die (the death rate) changes. The number of people moving into or out of an area (migration) also influences population change.

Now test yourself

10 Complete the 'population change' column in the table below by putting the following phrases in the correct place: little change; rapid increase; rapid decrease.

Birth rate	Death rate	Migration	Population change	Example
Few being born	Few die	Few move in or out		A developed country such as the UK
Many being born	Few die	Few move in or out	Rapid increase	A developing country such as Kenya
Many being born	Many die	Many moving in		A city in the developing world
Few being born	Few die	Many moving out		Rural areas of Britain

Now test yourself

People's attitudes to family size is one of the factors that controls the birth rate. Again, we can compare the opinions of a typical family from the developed world with one from a developing country.

Study the cartoons above.

11 Suggest two reasons why families in developed countries generally have fewer children.

12 Why are children so important to parents in developing countries? Suggest two reasons.

13 What do the cartoons suggest about the standard of health care in the two countries?

Why people move

The total number of people moving into or out of an area can also affect the size of the population. **Migration** can take place within a country or between two countries; over long distances or short distances; it can be temporary (for a short period of time) or permanent.

A **migrant** is the term used to describe someone who moves from place to place. An **immigrant** is someone who moves into an area and an **emigrant** is someone who moves out. Some people may move because they want to, while others may be forced out of their homes.

Now test yourself

14 Below are listed some of the reasons why people move. Copy the table, putting each reason in the correct column.

Reasons
wanting a new house   marriage
fear of persecution   retirement
nearer to friends and relatives
disease   famine   war
chance of job promotion
attractive area

A forced move	A move through choice

Case study: The Ernie Martin story

Ernie was born in India. During his life he has moved home on no less than eight occasions.

Year	From	To	Reason	Advantages
1962	India	Brighton, England	Whole family, including mother, father, two brothers and two sisters came to England	Make new friends and watch test cricket
1964	Brighton	Haywards Heath	Nurse's training	Opportunity for independence
1969	Haywards Heath	Edinburgh	Further training	Increase skills, so increases job opportunities
1972	Edinburgh	London	Advance in career	Closer to family in Brighton
1975	London	Brighton	Family reason	Family needed support
1975	Brighton	London	Career prospects	More responsible job
1979	London	Stafford	Aim to settle down with wife	Change of career focus. Now a job with a high profile
1988	Stafford	Boston, Lincolnshire	Promotion	Positive change of lifestyle; better for the family

Now test yourself

15 In an atlas, find a map of Britain. Try to locate each of the British towns Ernie has lived in.

16 How many times did Ernie move for (a) his career; (b) his family?

17 Do you think he likes living in Boston? Why?

Case study: Kurdish migration – a forced move?

In the early part of 1991, most of the Kurdish nation was 'on the move'. They were forced out from their homes because they felt their safety was being threatened by civil war.

Kurdistan had become part of the larger country of Iraq in 1922, but the Kurds never accepted themselves as Iraqis – they were Kurds first! Lack of co-operation between the Kurds and the Iraqi government has led to constant disagreement and occasional fighting.

At the end of the Gulf War, the Iraqi government decided to launch attacks against the Kurds. Many Kurds felt this was the last straw and the only option they had was to abandon their land and homes and flee across the mountains to Iran and Turkey.

Kurds on the move

In many cases Turkey felt that they could not cope with the millions of migrants flooding across the border. They simply did not have enough food or resources. The Kurds were grouped together in huge 'camps' on the mountainside with little food, no water and no sanitation. They just had to wait for politicians to decide their fate.

Fresh water is rare on such a move

'PLEASE DON'T SEND US BACK' BEG REFUGEES

Kurdish refugees yesterday pleaded with Foreign Office Minister Linda Chalker to save them from Saddam Hussein's clutches. Everyone she spoke to in the sprawling border camp at Isikveren, Turkey, told her they did not want to go back to Iraq – even if they are protected by Allied troops. Mothers held out their emaciated and filthy children as they begged Mrs Chalker for help, but one old man in traditional guerrilla gear shook her hand and said: 'Thank you Britain, thank you'. Another grabbed her arm and said, 'We can never go back while Saddam is still there. The best thing we want is to remove Saddam.' Patiently, Mrs Chalker told him, 'We understand that, but we must get you warm food and clothes and keep you strong.'

(From: The Daily Mirror)

Now test yourself

18 Copy the details below onto an outline map.

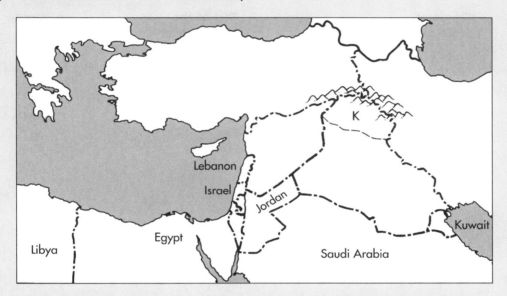

19 Use an atlas to find the four countries that border the area once called Kurdistan. Mark these on your map.

20 The area marked 'K' is where most of the Kurds live. Draw two arrows showing the direction of movement.

21 Why do you think the Kurds were forced to move?

22 List three problems they have faced on their journey.

23 Why do you think that the Kurds don't want to go back, as suggested by the newspaper article?

CHAPTER 12

Where people live

THE LOCATION OF SETTLEMENTS

The places where people live are called **settlements**. There are different types of settlements which have grown for different reasons. They may be small villages with houses and a few shops, or large towns with many houses, shopping centres, offices and factories.

By looking at the history of an area, we can often find out why some settlements began. An important clue is in the name of the settlement. The table gives some examples.

Origin of place name	Part of the place name	Meaning
Celts Originally from South Germany 2500–0 BC	Aber- } Inver- }	Mouth of
	Tre-	Town
	Pen-	Top of a hill
	Llan-	Church
	Pont-	Bridge
Romans Originally from Italy 0–400 AD	-caster } -chester } -cester }	Fort or castle
Saxons Originally from North Germany 400–600 AD	-borough } -bury }	Fort
	-ing	Group of people
	-ham	Homestead
	-ton	Enclosure
	-wich	Market
Vikings From Norway and Denmark 600–1000 AD	-by	Enclosure
	-ey	Island
	-dale	Valley
	-thorpe	Smaller village
	-ford	River crossing

We call the place where a settlement is built the **site**. Again, history can give us a clue as to why settlements grew where they did.

- **Defensive** sites are often found on hills or in the loop of a river bend. Early sites were often chosen because they were easy to defend against attacks from enemies.
- **Bridging points** were good sites for a settlement. Rivers could only be crossed at certain places where it was possible to build a bridge.
- **Wet-point** sites next to streams or springs were good sites for a settlement. Water was just as essential in those days.

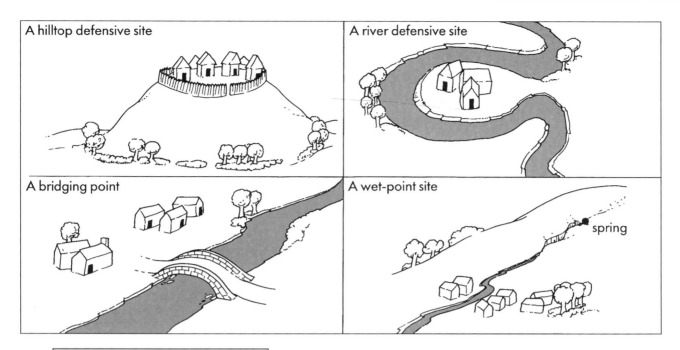

Now test yourself

1   Find a map of Britain in an atlas. Using the place name table, list examples of four Celtic, four Roman, four Saxon and four Viking settlements.

2

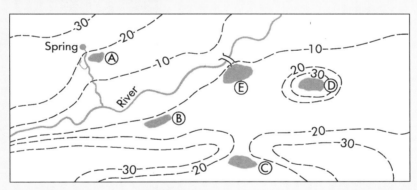

The map above shows five settlements (indicated by letters), whose **site** has been influenced by the landscape. Match the reasons for setting up with the letters:
dry points (away from flood risk); gap between two hills (good for transport); defensive; wet point; bridging point.

3   Copy the diagram above.
Shade in blue the area of the map most likely to be flooded.
Join each of the towns with a main road (the road has to cross over the bridge)

(a) Which town is most likely to grow into the largest settlement? Why?
(b) Which settlement is likely to have a castle? Why?

SETTLEMENT PATTERNS: THE SHAPE OF TOWNS

The shape that all the buildings in a town make is called a **settlement pattern**. The settlement pattern is usually affected by the slope of the land around it.

A dispersed pattern (spread out)

A **dispersed** pattern of settlement is found in areas where the people need a lot of land (such as in farming areas) or if the land is hilly so that only a few buildings can be built.

A linear pattern (straight line)

A **linear** pattern of settlement (straight line) is found in a valley where the steep valley sides prevent the growth of the town. Linear settlements may also be found along roads.

A nucleated pattern (close together)

A **nucleated** pattern of settlement is found where buildings in a town are built around a central point. This pattern is often found on flat lowland areas, when in the past, houses were built close to each other for protection.

Now test yourself

4   Which of the settlements labelled A, B and C
    on the sketch map is:
    nucleated; dispersed; linear?

5   What is in the centre of settlement C?

6   Give one reason why settlement A has developed
    in this way.

7   What is the most likely occupation of the owners
    of the houses in settlement B?

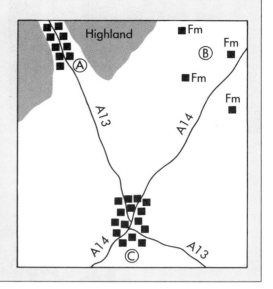

FUNCTIONS OF TOWNS

When a settlement is begun there has to be a reason for that settlement to grow.
This reason is called a **function**. The function is the main purpose of a settlement.
There are different types of functions.

*   **Market towns** began when much of the population were farmers. The farmers
    needed somewhere to sell their produce and where they could also buy things
    they needed, such as tools, seeds and anvils.
*   **Administration centres** deal with all the work involved in running a large area,
    such as a county. There are many offices here such as the County Hall, police
    headquarters and law courts.
*   **Holiday resorts** are places that people visit for holidays. The main function of a
    resort is to provide a place where people can enjoy themselves and relax.
*   **Ports** are places where goods can be brought into the country or sent to other
    countries by ship. Goods which are brought into a port are called **imports**,
    while goods sent out from a port are called **exports**.
*   **Industrial centres** mainly grow around factories producing goods. Other indus-
    trial towns may be based around a coal mine. These settlements are usually not
    as old as market towns.

A market town

An administration centre

A resort

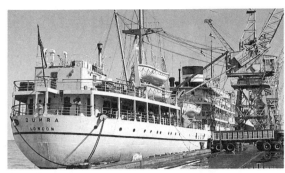

A port

An industrial centre

Now test yourself

8   Match the correct letter shown on the map with the correct function listed: port; administration centre; resort; market centre; industry.

9   There are three industrial towns. Which ones would contain:
(a) coal mine (b) glass works (uses sand) (c) brick works (uses clay)?

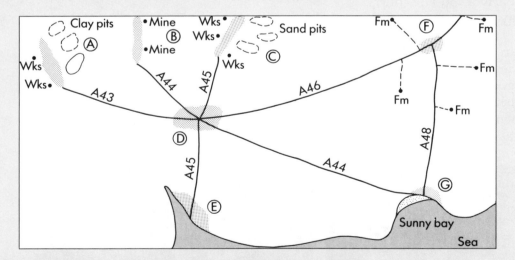

10   Which town is likely to contain the only sports centre of the area? Why?

11   Where would you locate a fun fair? Why?

12   Which town is likely to contain a centre for agricultural machinery? Why?

13   Tesco plans to build a large superstore in the area. Near which town do you think would be the best location? Why?

SETTLEMENT HIERARCHY: WHERE TO SHOP?

Some settlements are more important than others because of their functions. A settlement hierarchy is a way of putting settlements into order of importance.

The main way of deciding which settlements are more important is to look at the goods and services provided.

- **Low order** goods and services are needed every day, e.g. groceries, newspapers.
- **Middle order** goods and services are needed less frequently, perhaps once or twice a month, e.g. banks, clothing.
- **High order** goods and services are required less often, perhaps only once or twice a year or less, e.g. jewellers, opticians, furniture, electrical goods. Usually, most people are prepared to travel further, or make a special journey to obtain high order goods.

The settlements that provide these goods and functions can be classified in the same way.

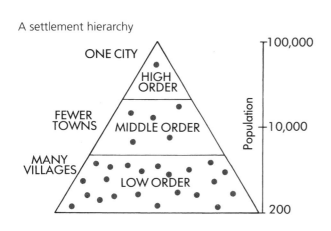

A settlement hierarchy

Settlement hierarchy in part of Yorkshire

Key:
- ◉ High order
- ○ Middle order
- • Low order

Settlement	Goods and services provided	Order
Hamlet	Small shop, maybe no services at all.	Low
Village	Small shop, post office, church, maybe small primary school.	Low
Small town	Several shops, supermarkets, banks, doctors, dentist.	Middle
Large town	Shopping centre, several supermarkets, jewellers, clothing and shoe shops.	Middle
City	Electrical goods, solicitors, shopping complexes, large hospital, cinemas, theatres.	High

Now test yourself

Fieldwork/enquiry

14 Plan, carry out and follow up a shopping questionnaire. This involves asking people their opinions of certain aspects of shopping. We can use a questionnaire to find out which town is the place most people go to when they want to shop for certain things.

Planning a questionnaire:

- design questions that are short, sharp and to the point;
- plan to go into a shopping centre to interview people/shoppers;
- choose a busy day when there are lots of people around to ask;
- it is sometimes helpful to wear a badge with your name and the name of your school clearly labelled.

During the questionnaire:

- when stopping people in the street, always remember to be polite – people are very busy and if they stop they will be helping *you*;
- work in groups of no more than two or three;
- you will need to ask at least 20 people, this gives a balanced view.

The questionnaire:

'Excuse me, I'm doing a school study about where people shop for certain things. Would you mind answering a few simple questions for me? It won't take too much time.'

1 In which town or village do you live?

2 How often do you come to this town? (Daily/weekly/monthly/infrequently)

3 In which town or village would you buy the following goods: groceries; newspapers; clothes; shoes; jewellery; furniture?

4 To which town or village would you go if you needed to use a: bank; solicitor; dentist; cinema?

'Thank you very much for your co-operation.'

(You may want to design your own questionnaire)

After the questionnaire:

- collect all the data together, look at it very carefully and see if there is a pattern in where people shop – can you work out which is the most important town?

HOW SMALL SETTLEMENTS CHANGE THROUGH TIME

Case study: Minehead

The town of Minehead is situated on the edge of the Exmoor National Park. Its origins date back to the eleventh century when it was an agricultural settlement, but it became more important as a port during the sixteenth century. A fire in 1791 destroyed the centre of Minehead, which was then rebuilt. As the port declined, the tourist trade grew with the attraction of nearby Exmoor. Today Minehead is a family resort. It has the added attraction of 'Somerwest World', formerly a Butlin's holiday camp, which can cater for up to 10 000 people – doubling the population of Minehead in the summer.

There are currently plans to restructure part of the sea front at Minehead with houses, flats and holiday apartments. The proposed site is a disused lido (swimming and recreational area) with the surrounding land. Almost 300 new dwellings are planned.

Local people are divided in their opinion of the development. Some people think that the town needs more high quality housing. Others believe that the land could be better used for recreational facilities for the town, because those at Somerwest World are too expensive for the locals.

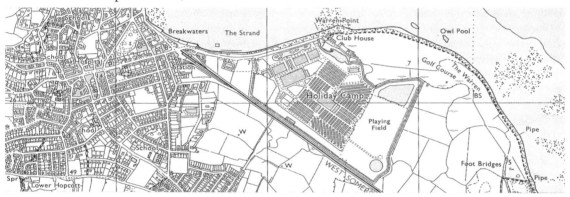

Now test yourself

£16m Seafront Housing Plan

Details of a £16 million proposal to restructure Minehead's eastern seafront with houses, flats, luxury holiday apartments and a sheltered housing scheme was revealed by the Rank Organisation this week, putting Minehead among the forefront of Britain's seaside resorts.

As the giant holiday company ended months of speculation, town and district councillors welcomed the investment in a holiday town which has been hamstrung this year by the dilapidated condition of the seafront lido site and the 'road to nowhere' status of the new seafront relief road which stopped short at the Somerwest World holiday centre.

Now all the wrangling is over and on Wednesday, George Rushton of Rank holiday and leisure division announced: 'I am pleased to say that we have reached agreement with county and district councils over the road and we will not only be dedicating the land but also will make a significant contribution towards the cost of constructing and completing the road.'

The sum of £165 000 has been speculated as the probable contribution by Rank, but Mr Rushton would not commit himself to a figure. He said construction should be completed over the winter of 1990/91.

He made it plain that this agreement for the completion of the road depends upon district planners giving the go-ahead to Rank's plans for developing the 11-acre lido site, which has lain derelict since they acquired it 5 years ago, and 2 adjoining acres now occupied by the Arnold Palmer Leisure Centre, which at present provides such amusements as crazy golf and go-karting.

It is unlikely that Rank will encounter any planning difficulties, but district planning officer Colin Russell said that such a comprehensive scheme would need careful investigation and it would be some three months before a decision could be finalised.

The plan for providing almost 300 new dwellings includes 36 terraced or semi-detached houses, 80 luxury seafront flats and 102 sheltered homes, all for sale.

(From: The Somerset County Gazette, 24 November 1989)

The proposed site

Read the article above and use your own knowledge to answer the following questions:

15 (a) What are the advantages for local people of the planned redevelopment?
    (b) Are there any disadvantages?

16 Do you think it will help the tourist trade? If so, how?

URBAN ZONES: DIFFERENT AREAS WITHIN TOWNS

As towns have grown in size, their original reason for being at a particular site has been lost. Development brings with it different functions. Large towns and cities that have grown from first settlements now have more than one function – usually shops and offices (commerce), housing (residential), factories (industry) and parks and playing fields (recreation).

You may have noticed when travelling through different towns that they resemble each other in the way they are laid out. For example, the main shopping areas are found in the centre, the style and age of the housing seems to get more modern as you move towards the edges of the town, and any industries are usually found together. If we look closely at the layout of towns it is possible to identify areas or **zones**. The diagram overleaf shows an example of a model town. Each ring shows a zone.

In order to prevent towns and cities from growing too large and taking up even more land, a law was passed which enabled town and city councils to set up a **green belt** around the town. This meant that building and development is strictly controlled in the green belt. This has been successful in some cases in stopping too much growth, but in other places developers have built on the land beyond the green belt, so that the green belt is almost another zone of the town.

Zone 1

The town centre or **central business district** (CBD). Many shops, banks and restaurants are found here. The bus station and train station are found here. Many different businesses would like to locate here. Land is expensive, so buildings are tall with several floors. There are few houses.

Zone 2

This area of the town was built in the last century. Then, it would have been full of factories and small terraced houses for the workers. Today this area is called the inner city. Many of the factories have been demolished, modernised or replaced.

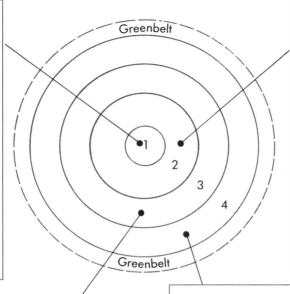

Zone 3

This zone is nearly all residential. The large houses would have been built in the 1920s and 1930s. We call this area the inner suburbs.

Zone 4

This is the newest part of the town. Here there are modern housing estates and some council estates. You will also find small, modern factories here and some large 'out-of-town' superstores. There are more parks and open spaces. The land is cheaper here.

Now test yourself

Fieldwork/enquiry

Make a journey from the edge of your nearest town into the town centre. Things to look for are listed below.

- Are there any changes in the age of the houses?
- Do you notice any changes in the size of the houses?
- Do you pass any factories – what are they like, old or new?
- Does the amount of open space change as you move into the town centre?
- Where do the houses stop and offices and shops start?
- Are there any buildings that have more than one storey, if so, where?

17 Try to draw a diagram of your journey into town.

18 Locate the CBD and see if you can identify the zones labelled in the model.

19 Does your town fit this model?

URBAN DEVELOPMENT

Towns and cities do not stay the same as time passes. Some parts are modernised and renewed, while others fall into disrepair and decay. What causes areas in a town to change?

- Town centres are popular areas for business, so need to be modernised to attract people.
- Industry may move to bigger or more modern factories.

- Older, terraced houses are small and need more money spent on them to keep them in good repair.
- Sometimes whole sections of towns can fall into disrepair because the original function has declined.

The renewel or modernisation of towns and cities is called **redevelopment**. Large-scale redevelopment is taking place in the dockland areas of London and Cardiff. As the importance of the docks declined large areas of these cities were left derelict. Modernisation has created new offices, modern industrial units and luxury apartment blocks.

Case study: Cardiff Bay redevelopment

In 1890, Cardiff was a thriving port. It exported coal from South Wales all over the world. Since then its importance has gradually declined until by the 1950s and 1960s large areas of former docklands had become derelict. In the 1980s, a 10-year development plan was proposed to regenerate the Cardiff Bay area.

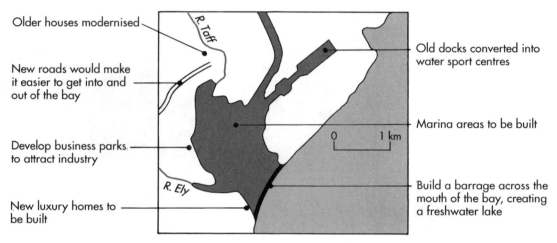

Proposed redevelopment in Cardiff Bay

The scheme was finally given the go-ahead from Parliament in 1994. A number of problems had to be overcome.

- Local houses may be prone to flooding as groundwater may rise into their cellars.
- Sewage coming down the River Taff may not be allowed out to sea.
- Large areas of mudflats will be destroyed so birds will not be able to feed.
- House prices may shoot up so local people will not be able to afford them.

Derelict docklands

Cardiff Bay at high tide

Now test yourself

Emily lives with her mum, dad, brother and two sisters in an area of Cardiff likely to be affected by the Cardiff Bay redevelopment. Like most of her neighbourhood, Emily is against the scheme. Her dad holds a different view.

Emily says: **Her father says:**

Local communities will break up due to all the newcomers buying expensive houses.

At present at low tide it looks awful. If the scheme goes ahead it will be more pleasing to the eye.

It may cause flooding.

It needs drastic action to clean the river. If they build the barrage the river will have to be kept clean.

There is no reason to destroy the wildlife areas.

Development should go on in peaceful ways and not be imposed upon people.

Lower Cardiff needs to be developed. Growth may go to other areas, destroying the environment and leading to the growth of other towns.

The quality of water in the river may deteriorate.

Many people are against it because they are concerned about the value of their property.

20 Read Emily's comments above. List three things that concern her about the barrage.

21 List three benefits Emily's father thinks the building of the barrage will bring to Cardiff.

22 If you lived in Cardiff would you be for or against the scheme? Give reasons for your answer.

Artist's impression of the Cardiff Bay barrage

PROBLEMS FOUND IN TOWNS

Too much traffic!

Traffic jams are common in many towns and cities. Nowadays there are so many cars, buses, vans and lorries trying to use the roads, that traffic congestion in towns is a frequent occurrence.

This increase in traffic and associated problems is because:

- older houses do not have garages, so cars are parked on the streets;
- nowadays people own more cars;
- many businesses prefer to use road transport rather than rail;
- there has been a large increase in the number of company cars;
- the number of lorries using the roads has also increased;
- people prefer to travel by car, as public transport can be slow, unreliable and expensive;

- town centres were built before cars were invented, so streets are often narrow, with many road junctions;
- road works and repairs can disrupt normal traffic flows.

Traffic problems are particularly bad during 'rush hours' – the times when many people are travelling to and from work. Too much traffic can lead to a number of problems:

- pollution from exhaust fumes can be a health risk, as well as causing damage to buildings;
- traffic is very noisy and can cause windows to shake;
- people caught in the traffic jams waste time, which may cost businesses money and can be frustrating for drivers;
- heavy traffic can lead to an increase in accidents.

Now test yourself

23 Conduct a survey in your class.
   (a) How many ride in a car at least once a day?
   (b) How many use public transport at least once a day?

24 Look at the line graph opposite, which shows traffic flow in a town centre.

   Describe and account for the pattern shown by the graph.

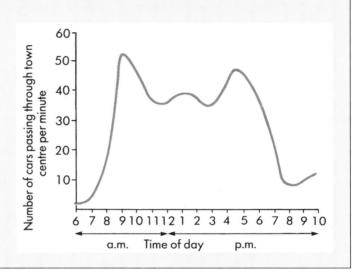

Are there solutions to the problem?

There are basically two ways of reducing the amount of traffic in town centres.

Either:

Introduce traffic management schemes to help the traffic move more easily through or around the town centre. The problem with many of these schemes is that:

- they are usually expensive;
- they use up more valuable land in the town centre;
- they encourage people to use their cars even more.

Or:

Make it very difficult and expensive for traffic to move around and through the town so that people will be encouraged to leave their cars at home. The problem with this approach is that:

- people are so used to the convenience of cars that it would probably take a lot of persuasion to change their attitudes.

A one-way system helps traffic move more easily through a town centre

'Sleeping policemen' on a road in Cardiff help to slow down the traffic

Now test yourself

25 Copy the table below.

Would lead to **more** cars in the town	Would lead to **less** cars in the town

26 Now put each of these traffic management schemes into the right column.
  (a) Introduce one-way systems.
  (b) Make public transport more reliable, comfortable and frequent.
  (c) Build a multi-storey car park in the town centre.
  (d) Increase the price of petrol and make fares on public transport very cheap.
  (e) Build a by-pass around the town.
  (f) Restrict movement in town centres by pedestrianising shopping areas.
  (g) Give priority to buses and bicycles in town centres.
  (h) Build a series of roundabouts at problem junctions.
  (i) Cut down on the number of car parking spaces and increase charges.
  (j) Introduce traffic lights.

Where to build a by-pass?

Sometimes a by-pass may be the only solution to a particular traffic problem. For example, Little Dollington is a village with a busy main road running straight through the middle of it. The road is used by hundreds of lorries every day, going to and coming from the local quarry.

Why is a by-pass needed?

'My children's school is right on the main road. They have to cross it at the busiest times of day. I'm worried that there will be a serious accident one day.'
(A young mother)

'I have to drive through Little Dollington every day. It adds at least 20 minutes onto my journey and I only have to go a few miles. I use lots of fuel and spend most of my time stuck in a traffic jam.'
(A lorry driver)

'My shop is in the High Street. There is so much dirt from the traffic that I can't display my produce outside. My delivery lorries have trouble unloading and customers won't cross the busy road.'
(A greengrocer)

'I live on the main road. Every time a lorry goes past my windows rattle! I can't hang washing out – it comes off the line dirty. In the summer I can't open my windows because of the fumes and noise.'
(A local resident)

Choosing a route for a by-pass is never easy. There are many things that have to be taken into account.

Now test yourself

27 Look at the sketch map below which shows three possible by-pass routes round Little Dollington. Each one has its problems. Describe the problems associated with each of the routes.

28 The by-pass will cost a quarter of a million pounds for every kilometre. Which route will be the cheapest?

29 Which route do you think should be chosen and why?

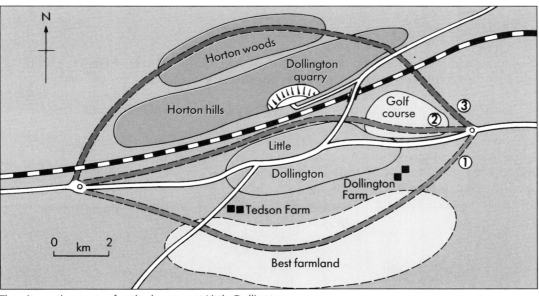

The alternative routes for the by-pass at Little Dollington

CHAPTER 13

*E*conomic activity

C OMPETITION FOR LAND

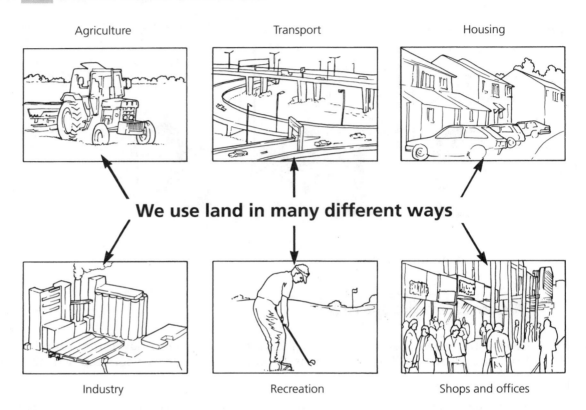

Agriculture

Transport

Housing

We use land in many different ways

Industry

Recreation

Shops and offices

We use land in many different ways. Some activities require a large amount of land, while others need only a small area. If a piece of land is in a desirable location, several companies may compete to own it. If there are many people interested in buying a piece of land, it becomes more valuable and its price goes up.

Now test yourself

1   Do the following activities require large or small areas of land: a golf course; a farm; a sports centre; a shoe shop; an industrial complex; a house; a three-lane motorway; an airport?

2   Which two of the following phrases, if true, would lead to an increase in land values (the other two would lead to a decrease)?
    (a) Barratts building a housing estate on poor quality farmland.
    (b) The local council giving permission for a waste disposal site nearby.
    (c) Breaching of a sea wall, increasing the risk of flooding.
    (d) Building a link road, increasing accessibility.

PRIMARY ACTIVITY

An example of primary activity is farming. Farmland can be used in a variety of ways:

- **arable farming** is where farmers grow crops such as wheat and barley;
- **pastoral farming** is where farmers look after animals such as dairy cows or sheep;
- **mixed farming** is where crops and animals are farmed.

Farming can be done in large buildings such as greenhouses, chicken houses or stalls.

Some farming terms are given below:

- **permanent pasture** is where fields are always kept as grass and used as pasture land for animals;
- **silage** is grass that is cut green and kept to feed animals in winter;
- **ley grass** is grass that is planted, fields with ley grass are occasionally ploughed up;
- **crop rotation** is when different crops are grown in each field every year, as part of a cycle.

Case study: Coed Morgan Farm

Coed Morgan Farm is a dairy farm in south-east Wales. Mr Meadmore, the farmer, also grows some cereal crops (known as fodder crops) most of which he feeds to his animals in winter. He also keeps some beef cattle and some sheep.

Facts and figures	
Number of hectares	74
Workers – Full-time	2
– Part-time	1
Dairy cows	62
Beef cattle	107
Sheep	200
Lambs	200

The farmer's income

Milk	50%	Beef	32%
Cereals	10%	Sheep	8%

The fodder crops Mr Meadmore grows are grown in the same field over a 10-year period in rotation. Ley grass is grown for five years in this cycle to allow the fields to regain their fertility.

Year	1	2	3	4	5	6	7	8	9	10
Crop	Wheat	Maize	Oats	Wheat	Barley	Ley grass ⟶				

How Mr Meadmore uses his land

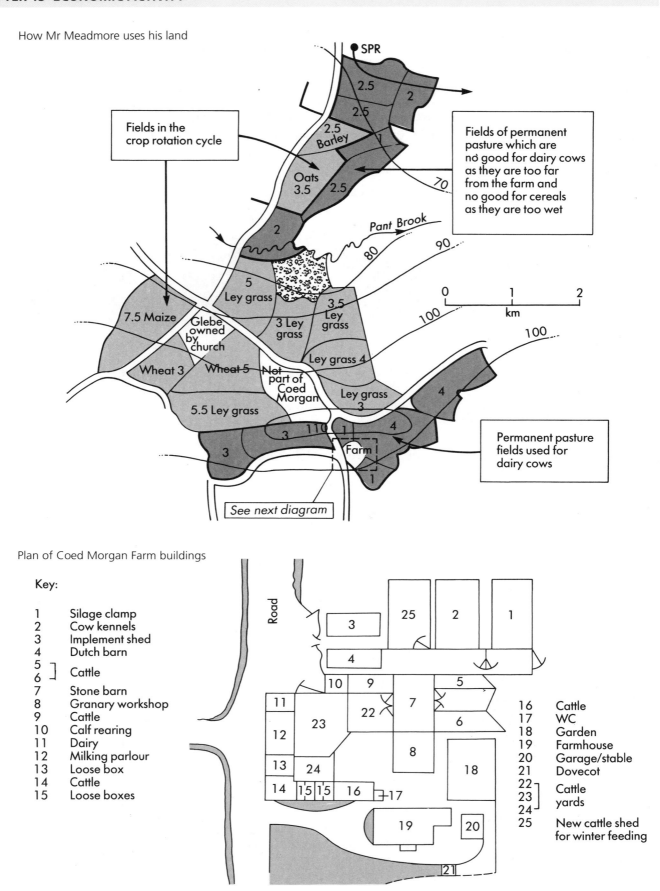

Fields in the crop rotation cycle

Fields of permanent pasture which are no good for dairy cows as they are too far from the farm and no good for cereals as they are too wet

Permanent pasture fields used for dairy cows

See next diagram

Plan of Coed Morgan Farm buildings

Key:

1 Silage clamp
2 Cow kennels
3 Implement shed
4 Dutch barn
5 ⎤
6 ⎦ Cattle
7 Stone barn
8 Granary workshop
9 Cattle
10 Calf rearing
11 Dairy
12 Milking parlour
13 Loose box
14 Cattle
15 Loose boxes

16 Cattle
17 WC
18 Garden
19 Farmhouse
20 Garage/stable
21 Dovecot
22 ⎤
23 ⎥ Cattle
24 ⎦ yards
25 New cattle shed for winter feeding

Now test yourself

3   Name four dairy products.

4   The fields furthest from the farm are not suitable for dairy cows. Why do you think this is so?

5   (a) What is crop rotation?
    (b) Why does the farmer grow grass for five years in succession?

6   Use the table labelled 'The farmer's income' on page 123 to draw a pie chart.
    Hint: Pie charts are useful to show percentages (see page 18).
    Each circle-graph is 360° all round, so to draw a portion of the circle to show a percentage,
    we use a simple calculation, e.g.
    every 1% = 3.6°, so 10% = 10 × 3.6 = 36°.

Problems facing dairy farmers

During the 1960s and 1970s, dairy farmers were encouraged to produce as much milk as they could. They increased the size of their herds and many took out bank loans to buy more grazing land. This resulted in overproduction and the creation of butter mountains.

In 1984, the government introduced dairy quotas. A quota is a limit on the amount a farmer can produce – a heavy fine is imposed if farmers exceed their quota. Dairy farmers were forced to cut their herds and cut down on the amount of milk produced. Many cows were slaughtered and many millions of gallons of milk were poured down the drain. In an effort to supplement their incomes, farmers have been forced into diversification. This means using their land in other ways, this has included:

*   growing cereals or keeping other animals rather than dairy cattle;
*   attracting tourists by converting farm buildings into holiday cottages and/or offering bed and breakfast;
*   offering educational visits and nature trails;
*   providing sporting activities, e.g. golf ranges, pony trekking or mountain biking;
*   growing soft fruits and inviting the public to 'pick-your-own'.

S ECONDARY ACTIVITY

A large proportion of land in Britain is given over to industry. Some industries require large areas of land, while others need only enough land on which to build a small factory. Industrial complexes can cover several square miles, such as the ICI plant on Teesside. Smaller factories are mainly grouped together on industrial estates or in business parks.

A steelworks

An industrial estate

The advantages of locating similar activities together

Lots of factories are usually found together on a trading estate. They are not there by accident. Each factory takes advantage of a particular set of circumstances, as shown in the diagram.

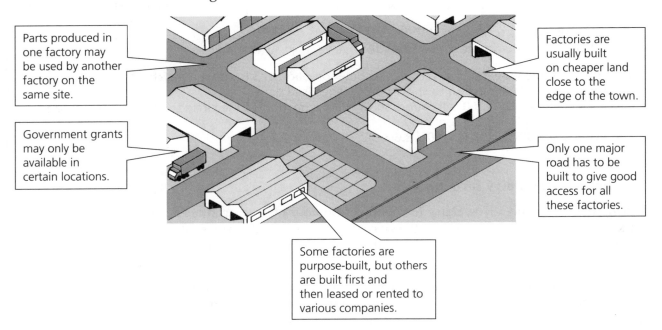

Parts produced in one factory may be used by another factory on the same site.

Government grants may only be available in certain locations.

Factories are usually built on cheaper land close to the edge of the town.

Only one major road has to be built to give good access for all these factories.

Some factories are purpose-built, but others are built first and then leased or rented to various companies.

Why industry comes and goes

Case study: The iron and steel story in South Wales

During the 19th century iron and steel works grew up on the South Wales Coalfield where iron ore, limestone and coal were found. These are the **raw materials** for iron and steel production. They are very heavy products that are difficult and expensive to transport. It was much easier and cheaper to make iron and steel close to the raw material. There used to be many small ironworks (35 in all), each producing small quantities of iron.

Ironworks and raw materials in 1861

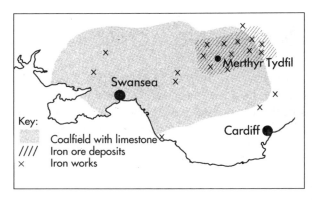

Key:
- Coalfield with limestone
- //// Iron ore deposits
- × Iron works

Nowadays, steelworks are found on the coast. This is because the iron ore in Wales is expensive to mine and the best quality ore has already been used. It is now cheaper to import iron ore from abroad. It is still heavy and expensive to transport, so a location near to a port is best. Today there are only two large, modern steelworks in Port Talbot and Llanwern using the most advanced technology to produce steel.

Steelworks and raw materials in 1991

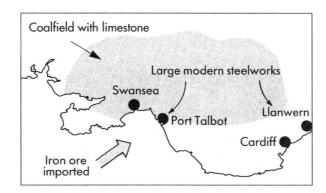

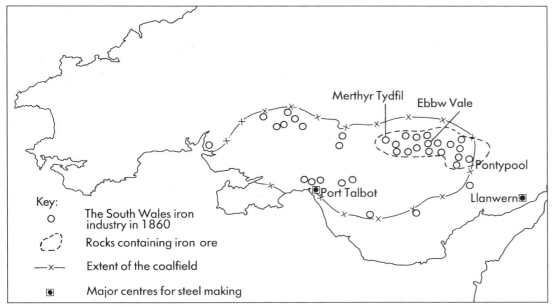

Key:
○ The South Wales iron industry in 1860
⌐‿⌐ Rocks containing iron ore
—×— Extent of the coalfield
◙ Major centres for steel making

Now test yourself

7 Give two reasons why ironworks were located 'on the coalfields' in 1861.

8 What is meant by the term 'raw materials'?

9 Give two reasons why steelworks are located on the coast nowadays.

10 Why do you think there are only two steelworks operating now in South Wales?

Why economic activities develop in particular locations

Case study: The M4, South Wales

As farming has become less profitable some farmers have begun to sell off their land to the highest bidder. The land next to motorway junctions is very desirable for industrial use because nowadays people and goods have to be able to travel quickly. For these reasons a variety of economic activities has sprung up between junctions 33 and 35 of the M4 in South Wales.

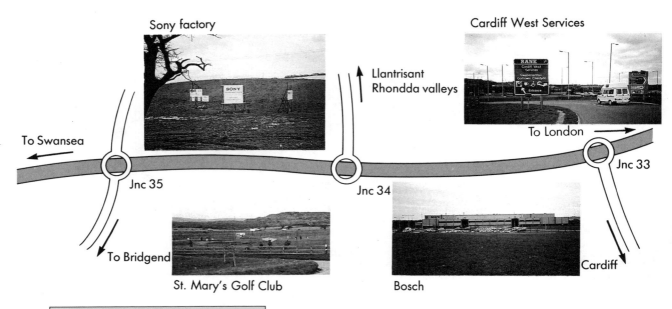

Sony factory

Cardiff West Services

To Swansea

Jnc 35

Llantrisant
Rhondda valleys

Jnc 34

To London →

Jnc 33

To Bridgend

St. Mary's Golf Club

Bosch

Cardiff

Now test yourself

11 Give two reasons why the M4 motorway junction is a good location for these businesses.

TERTIARY ACTIVITY

Shoe shops – middle order goods

An example of a tertiary activity is a shoe shop. In any High Street, shoe shops can often be found next door to each other. The reason is that shoes are an example of middle order goods. People do not buy shoes every day, so they would be prepared to make a special journey to buy them. They are also **comparison** goods. People will compare prices and styles before deciding on which pair to buy. It is therefore an advantage to have such shops together – people do not want to walk long distances between shops.

Now test yourself

The sketch map shows the location of five shoe shops in a High Street.

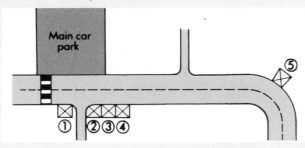

You go into town by car to buy a pair of shoes.

12 Which of the shoe shops are you likely to visit first? Why?
13 Are you likely to buy the first pair of shoes you try on? Why/why not?
14 Which of the shoe shops is more likely to do the least amount of business? Why?

HOW SUPERSTORES USE LAND

Superstores are also a tertiary activity. The layout of a superstore is carefully planned out to benefit both the customer and the store personnel.

A plan view of a typical store

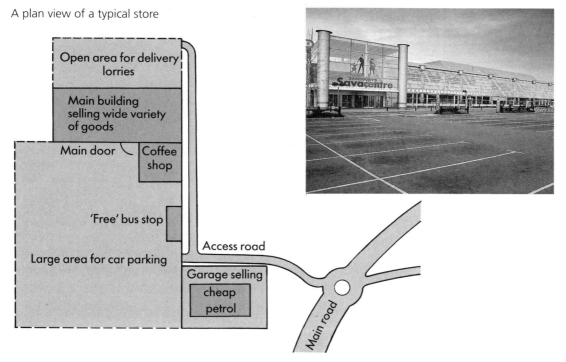

Now test yourself

Look carefully at the plan and the photograph above.

15 What attractions are there for the motorist?

16 Why should deliveries only take place at the back of the store?

17 Do you have to own a car to use this store? Why?

18 Give two reasons why being next to a main road is very important for the store.

TOURISM

Tourism is the industry that caters for people who want a holiday. Nearly 60% of people living in the European Community took a holiday of some kind during 1991. Tourism is, therefore, a major industry. It provides jobs for about 18 million people across Europe. Places people visit for a holiday are called resorts.

The tourism industry has grown rapidly over the last 30 years. This is because:

- people have more leisure time from working shorter hours, having paid leave from their work or simply retiring at a younger age;
- people have become richer, so they have more money to spend on luxuries such as holidays;
- more information is available about other places, so people want to visit them;
- it is easier to get to places that were once considered far away;
- a full range of purpose-built resorts and package holidays has become available.

There are different types of holiday, and therefore each tourist area can offer a different range of facilities and activities and so attract a different type of tourist.

- Long-stay summer resorts attract people who want to spend a week or more in one centre. These resorts are usually found on the coast where there are sandy beaches and, often, warm dry summers.
- Short-stay attractions are usually visited by people on day trips or short breaks. These places have to be easy to reach.
- Cultural and historical centres tend to be in towns and cities where the visitors are people who are interested in architecture, art and history.
- Skiing has become very popular in the winter in the last twenty years. Mountain walking and scenic views also attract many visitors during the summer.

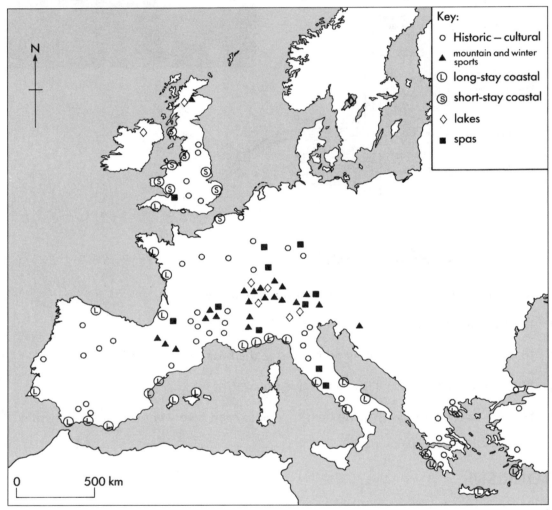

Tourist areas of Europe

Now test yourself

19 List six jobs associated with tourism. Think about how people book holidays, the places where they stay and how they travel there.

20 What sort of facilities would a resort require for *you* to have an enjoyable holiday?

21 Find out where your friends went on holiday. What did they do when they got there? Was it very different from your holiday experience?

22 Look at the map of Europe, above. Name the five countries that have long-stay coastal resorts by looking at an atlas. Why do you think there are so many resorts in these countries?

23 Why are there so few long-stay resorts in northern Europe?

Holidays in Britain

Despite the attractions of a foreign holiday, many people still take their annual holiday in this country. Britain also attracts many foreign tourists, so tourism in the UK is a very important industry. It employs nearly 6% of the population and earns almost £10 billion per year.

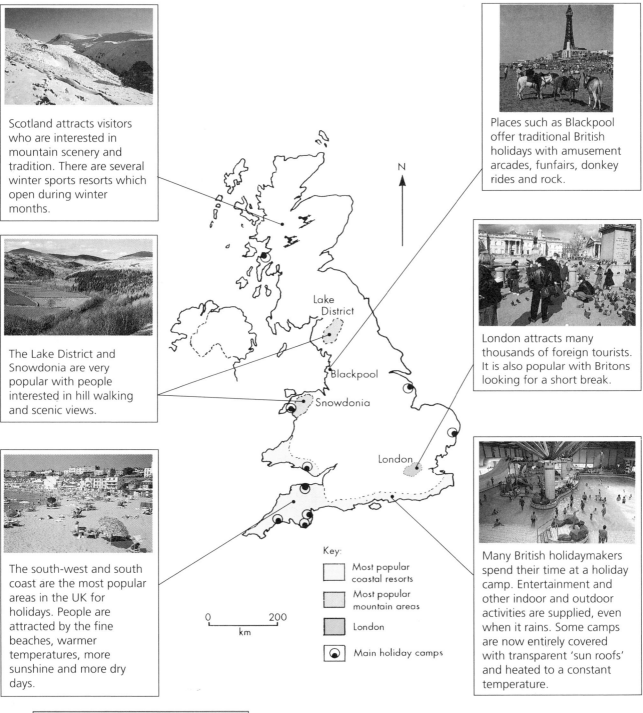

Scotland attracts visitors who are interested in mountain scenery and tradition. There are several winter sports resorts which open during winter months.

The Lake District and Snowdonia are very popular with people interested in hill walking and scenic views.

The south-west and south coast are the most popular areas in the UK for holidays. People are attracted by the fine beaches, warmer temperatures, more sunshine and more dry days.

Places such as Blackpool offer traditional British holidays with amusement arcades, funfairs, donkey rides and rock.

London attracts many thousands of foreign tourists. It is also popular with Britons looking for a short break.

Many British holidaymakers spend their time at a holiday camp. Entertainment and other indoor and outdoor activities are supplied, even when it rains. Some camps are now entirely covered with transparent 'sun roofs' and heated to a constant temperature.

Key:
- Most popular coastal resorts
- Most popular mountain areas
- London
- Main holiday camps

0   200
km

Now test yourself

24 Explain why many people are attracted to the south-west and south coast for their holiday.

25 Why do you think many foreign tourists spend at least some of their holiday in London?

26 What sort of people would be attracted to a holiday camp? Why?

27 Which of the holidays outlined above would be most suitable for an elderly couple? Why?

Tourism in Britain is not without its problems, for example:

- during peak holiday times, roads to resorts can become crowded and congested, making journeys a nightmare;
- small villages and holiday towns can get crowded during the summer but are extremely quiet out of season, this can make it difficult for hotels, restaurants and shops to stay in business;
- lack of business during the winter means unemployment for many tourism workers.

A summer beach scene in Cornwall

Brighton beach during winter

Many resorts are trying to minimise the problems by:

- trying to extend the season by keeping places of interest open longer and encouraging people to take short breaks;
- trying to attract business conferences to the town;
- opening all-season attractions, such as model villages, leisure centres and theatres.

Holidays in the sun

Many British people now take their holidays abroad. Holidays organised by travel agents and tour operators can be as cheap as holidays in Britain. Countries around the Mediterranean Sea have become very popular. Hot, dry weather throughout the summer is virtually guaranteed and with sandy beaches and a clear, warm sea to swim in this area of Europe is very appealing. It is also easy to get to the Mediterranean resorts, flights take 2 to 4 hours, the same time it may take to get to a British resort.

Case study: The Greek island of Kos

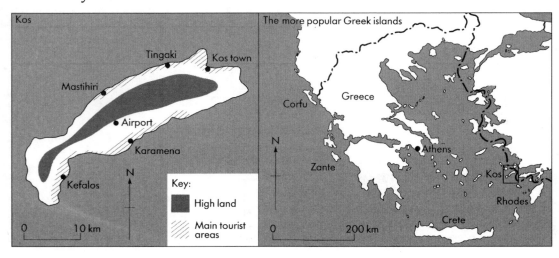

Climates compared

		April	May	June	July	Aug	Sep	Oct
Kos	Average temperature °C	20	23	26	30	29	27	24
	Sunshine hours	8	10	12	13	12	10	8
London	Average temperature °C	13	16	19	29	29	18	14
	Sunshine hours	5	6	7	6	6	5	4

Kos is one of the lesser known Greek Islands, although over the past ten years it has become increasingly popular with British tourists. It takes about 3 hours 50 minutes to fly there from Britain and the island offers a wide range of accommodation. It has the reputation of being very green and quiet. Its sandy beaches and a calm, warm, shallow sea make it an ideal location for families with young children. There are plenty of bars and tavernas (inns) where visitors can enjoy good food and traditional Greek dancing.

Tourists are not the only people on Kos. The island has a rich history and there have been people living and working there for centuries. However, tourism has brought a total change to the island. Tourists want to stay in good accommodation with electricity and running water, so drainage and sanitation have been improved. There has been a change in traditional occupations, too. Sadly, more people also means more noise, litter, pollution and crime.

Traditional Greek fishing boats

Greek culture and heritage

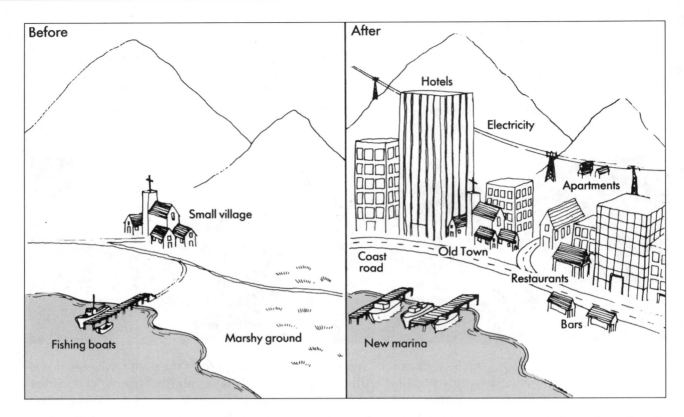

Occupations: farming using primitive methods growing olives and fruits, keeping a few goats; fishing in the rich waters off the island

Occupations: waiters, bar tenders, making local crafts, souvenir shops, taxi drivers, bus drivers, fishing trips, boat trips, watersports, cleaners, hotel staff

Now test yourself

28 Use an atlas to locate Kos. In which sea(s) is it found?

29 What are the attractions of Kos for the British tourist?

30 Use the climate figures to draw a bar graph showing the average temperature and average sunshine hours for Kos and London.

31 Look at the drawings, showing Kos before and after the island became a tourist centre, and list five ways in which tourism has changed the island.

Winter resorts

Since the late 1970s, winter sports holidays have been very popular in areas such as The Alps. This had led to a huge growth in the skiing industry and in the number of tour operators offering skiing holidays. A number of purpose-built resorts have sprung up throughout The Alps to ease the pressure on the more traditional resorts. Skiing is a very specialised activity and requires specialised facilities. Ski runs (pistes) have to be prepared, ski lifts installed, hotels built, medical facilities made available and other winter facilities provided, e.g. cross-country skiing, tobogganing and ice skating. These activities take place during the winter, when it gets dark early, so the resorts usually provide a range of après-ski (evening) activities.

Case study: Val Thorens, French Alps

SKI FACTS

High altitude and
glacier skiing
Snow cannons: 115
Artificial piste: 11.5 km
No. of lifts: 200
Km of piste: 600 km
Direction of slopes: SE, E, N, W
Mountain restaurants: 9
Easy runs: 101, Medium runs: 155
 Difficult runs: 28

Après-ski: At least 20 bars and
restaurants; fashion and food shops;
tennis and squash; cinema; three
discos

Now test yourself

Use all the information given to answer these questions.

32 Why has there been a need to build more winter sports resorts in The Alps?

33 What is meant by the terms:
 (a) specialised activity;
 (b) piste;
 (c) après-ski?

34 Val Thorens is a 'snow sure' resort.
 (a) What do you think this means?
 (b) Why is it important?

35 How do you think ski resorts change the natural environment?

Leisure and the land

Each year nearly 100 million people visit the **National Parks** of England and Wales. The National Parks are areas of 'outstanding natural beauty' which were identified by an Act of Parliament in the 1950s for special protection and public enjoyment. Although the name 'national park' suggests they belong to the nation, this is not the case. Most land is privately owned and is the livelihood of many of the owners.

The National Parks were set up to be enjoyed. But their very visitors can cause great damage – most of the time without realising it. The worst problem is that most visitors come at the same time, e.g. a warm Sunday afternoon during the summer. There is conflict between the different people who want to use the National Parks. The landowners need to use the land to make a living, but there are rules about what the land can be used for. Building is strictly controlled.

Different land use in Snowdonia: ramblers and farming

Conflicts between the land users in the National Parks

Visitor
I want to be able to walk across the fields. I need somewhere to stay. I need picnic areas and toilets. I need somewhere to park my car. I want to be able to drive around the National Park and go wherever I please!

Landowner
I need to use modern farming methods to make a decent living. I don't want tourists tramping over my land, leaving gates open, dropping litter and letting their dogs scare my animals.

National Park officer
I have to make sure the rules are followed. The natural beauty of the park must be preserved and the general public must be able to enjoy it. I have to meet local needs regarding development, small scale industry and agriculture. Visitors must have car parks, toilets and information centres. I also encourage volunteer groups to do conservation work.

Villager
My village is full of cars in the summer so there is too much noise and exhaust fumes. My son cannot afford to buy a house because city people push the prices up. I can't even build an extension or have the double glazing I want.

(represents the National Park Authority)

Case study: Exmoor

More than 80% of the 686 square kilometres of Exmoor is privately owned. Most of it is used for farming, especially sheep and beef cattle. The public has great freedom within Exmoor, as there are over 900 kilometres of footpath and bridleways. This freedom is because of the tolerance of the landowners – so long as the visitors respect the Countryside Code.

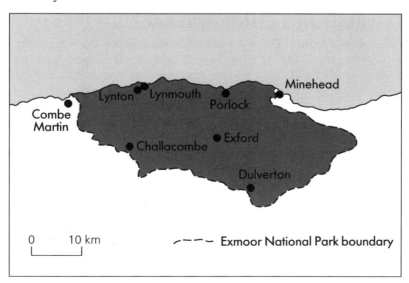

Now test yourself

Start anywhere on the left-hand side of this grid. What do the initials stand for? Look at the clues. See how quickly you can get across.

NPA The committee that controls the Parks
NPO The representative of the NPA
LO   80 per cent of Exmoor belongs to them
V   100 million each year in National Parks
B   Strictly controlled in National Parks
CP   Self-catering tourists stay here
C   Pitch your tent here
D   Town on Exmoor
HaC They wear away footpaths
CC   Rules of the countryside
G   Don't leave these open
CW   You can volunteer for this!
FaB For tourists on 2 legs or 4!
L   Don't drop it – take it home
EF   Too many cars cause this pollution
PS   Eat your lunch here
H   Not enough of these for local people
SaC Exmoor farmers rear these

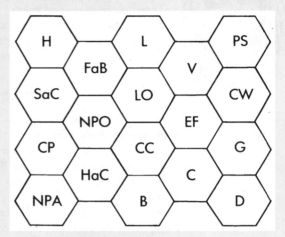

There are many problems on Exmoor, they include:

- farmers enclose the land so that it is inaccessible (a seventh is ploughed up or fenced off);
- hikers and climbers wear away footpaths;
- shortage of houses for local people – they cannot afford to pay the high prices paid by those who come from the city;
- more tourists prefer to self-cater, so they need more caravan parks and campsites;
- more cars means that more land has to be used for car parks;
- more visitors means more noise, more litter, more traffic jams and more of a danger to wildlife.

EXMOOR'S CHANGING FACE

Many visitors tend to have a romanticised view of the countryside and of the people who live there. But as any countryside dweller will tell you, it isn't always like that.

Here on Exmoor the cost of living has all but caught up with the rest of the UK. The same cannot be said of the local wages. Employment prospects have always been thin, in or out of recession, and for years many local youngsters have looked elsewhere for their future.

It is true that, nowadays, there are more jobs in tourism than in agriculture, but most are seasonal and unlikely to provide for full family support.

The influx of better-off people from away – usually to retire – affects the price of housing and thus the prospects of the local first-time homemaker. Shops, schools, health and recreation are becoming more centralised in the towns – the village school and shop are now rarities in the remoter communities – and public transport has become confined to the busier routes on the fringes of Exmoor.

Urban influences tend to prevail; and, as elsewhere, television is inevitably diluting the local culture.

The backbone of Exmoor's community still remains those who shape its landscape – the farmers and the landowners. Despite mechanisation, their work is no less hard than their ancestors'. But profit margins are low or non-existent and survival has been largely dependent on hill farming support grants. Now, with subsidies being constantly eroded, many Exmoor farmers face difficult times ahead.

(From: The Exmoor Visitor, March 1991)

CHAPTER 14

*U*sing the Earth's resources

NATURAL RESOURCES

The Earth is rich in natural resources. **Natural resources** are the things that are found within or on the Earth that can be used by humans. Natural resources can be grown on the land; caught in the sea; reared by farmers; mined or quarried. Natural resources differ from manufactured goods because they are not made in a factory. Natural resources can be divided into two types:

- **non-renewable** resources can be used only once, once they have gone, they have gone forever;
- **renewable** resources will not run out, provided they are not over-exploited.

People have become very concerned of late about how quickly we are using up the Earth's non-renewable resources. Many may run out (become exhausted) in the next 100 years. Although new reserves are found every day, sometimes they are not enough to cope with excessive use.

Resource	Year it runs out
Diamonds	2008
Silver	2010
Gold	2018
Oil	2025
Zinc	2028
Tin	2030
Lead	2036
Copper	2044

When resources will run out

Oil refinery

One way of prolonging the life of non-renewable resources is by recycling. Britain is way behind some of its European neighbours when it comes to recycling. Nevertheless, the number of bottle banks and paper recycling centres is increasing and people are gradually becoming more aware of recycling potential.

Product	% recycled in 1990
Steel	60%
Copper	40%
Aluminium	35%
Paper	33%
Glass	10%
Plastic	8%
Rubber	6%

Percentage of product recycled

Now test yourself

1 Are the following products renewable or non-renewable:
coal; wheat; fish; cotton; timber; iron ore?

2 Explain what is meant by the following words in Geography:
exhausted; reserves; recycling; resources; manufactured goods; raw material.

3 Match the correct manufactured item with its raw materials:

Raw material	Manufactured items
Cod	Wooden table
Iron ore	House brick
Gold	Railway rail
Wool	Fish finger
Timber	Sweater
Clay	Wedding ring

4 Construct a bar graph using the 'When resources will run out' table (see page 139).

How extracting resources can damage the environment
Case study: Coal

Coal is one of Britain's most important natural resources. It was coal that gave
Britain the power to develop its other resources during the Industrial Revolution.

The winding gear of an old colliery, used to be a typical feature of coal mining areas.

A hundred years ago, when coal mining was at its height, very little attention was
paid to the environment. It was the coal that was important and any waste was
simply dumped close to the mines. As more coal was mined, more waste was
dumped, until huge coal tips or spoil heaps could be seen. Today the coal mining
areas of Britain are scarred with these ugly remnants of past mining. Opencast
mining causes even more damage.

How coal tips damage the environment

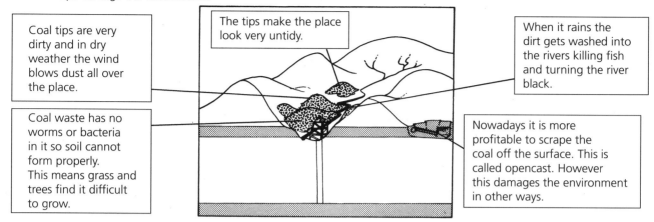

Coal tips are very dirty and in dry weather the wind blows dust all over the place.

The tips make the place look very untidy.

When it rains the dirt gets washed into the rivers killing fish and turning the river black.

Coal waste has no worms or bacteria in it so soil cannot form properly. This means grass and trees find it difficult to grow.

Nowadays it is more profitable to scrape the coal off the surface. This is called opencast. However this damages the environment in other ways.

The modern coal industry

During the early part of the 1990s the government's review of our energy requirements concluded that coal was not the fuel of the future. Since then the amount of coal mined and the number of collieries has been cut dramatically. Only the most efficient and profitable mines have remained open, as these are the only ones who can produce coal cheaply enough to compete with foreign imports.

A major factor in the government's decision was that the electricity generating companies could not guarantee that they would use as much coal in the future. Coal is perceived to be a dirty fuel. Smoke from chimney stacks leads to acid rain if not filtered properly, and filtering the smoke is an expensive business. In addition, large areas of land are needed next to the power station to store the coal. Alternative sources of power are now more readily available. At present gas-fired power stations are cleaner and cheaper, and can respond more quickly to the changes in demand for electricity.

As a result, many former coalmining areas have become zones of 'industrial blight'. For example, in South Wales the only coal produced today comes from privately-owned mines. There are no working mines owned by British Coal. Former mining areas have become economic 'blackspots' with high unemployment, falling living standards, out-migration, and an increasingly elderly population and ever decreasing local services. Business prospects are bleak so many shops have closed down. There is little chance of them re-opening and so they remain boarded up.

Can damaged landscapes be restored?

Once an environment has been polluted, it is very difficult to put it back to what it was before. It can be done, but it involves a lot of money, time, effort and a will to want to do it.

Reclaiming the land is an expensive business.
It takes many years for the landscape to look 'natural' again.

In some coal mining areas efforts are being made to 'reclaim' old coal tips. This involves:

- clearing the tip using heavy machinery – modern technology means that some of the coal that was dumped can now be burnt in our more efficient power stations;
- landscaping the area – the bulldozers can begin to put the land back to its original shape;
- fertilising the area and introducing worms and bacteria to help the soil form;
- spreading grass seed over the whole area.

Reclaimed coal tips in South Wales

Now test yourself

Improving the environment can be done on a very small scale. It does not have to involve a lot of time or expense. All it needs is a little bit of effort. For example, litter could be collected from a park or the school grounds.

5   Design an activity to improve a small part of your local environment.

6   Get a group of friends to help you carry out the task.

7   After you have completed it, ask yourself 'Have I really improved the environment?'

8   Think of ways to stop the problem occurring again.

Energy resources: if the price is right!

Case study: Oil in Alaska

Oil is an example of a non-renewable fossil fuel. That means it was formed many millions of years ago and once gone, it will never return.

The developed world has become increasingly dependent on oil. As oil has become more scarce, governments and oil companies are prepared to go anywhere in the world to search for it. As more oil has been used, its price has gone up and the desire to produce more has increased. Today it has become 'economically feasible' to exploit known oil reserves even in the most inhospitable parts of the world because of improvements in technology.

The facts

- Alaska is the northernmost state of the USA;
- the USA needed oil;
- in 1965, oil was found in vast amounts in Prudhoe Bay;
- there was a six-year delay on a decision to build a pipeline mainly because of environmental concerns;
- in 1977 the pipeline was completed;
- reserves should last for 50 years.

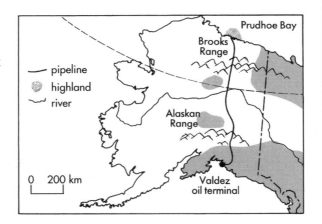

The problems

- oil was found in the north but was needed 400km to the south;
- Prudhoe Bay is frozen for 10 months of the year which is difficult for tankers;
- temperatures fall to 50°C in winter, often with blizzards;
- the ground is permanently frozen, making mining and building difficult;
- workers do not want to live in such a difficult environment, thousands of miles from their families;
- parts of Alaska are mountainous and prone to earthquakes.

The solution

- build a pipeline 1285km long from Prudhoe Bay in the north to Valdez in the south, overland for most of the way, to carry 1.2 million barrels of warm oil every day!

Alaskan oil has affected both the local people and the environment. Alaska is home to a wide variety of bird life. The pipeline represented a physical barrier to migrating caribou and underpasses were built.

The pipeline was built on stilts so that the warm oil would not melt the frozen ground. 600 streams and rivers were crossed, including spawning ground for salmon

Most Inuits (sometimes called Eskimos) who live in Alaska no longer live in the traditional manner (hunting whales and seals and living 'on the ice' in igloos). Most Inuits are now fully integrated into a 'westernised' culture. They now live in permanent settlements, eat western-style diets and many of them have jobs in the oil industry. When the outside world came to Alaska it changed their traditional society, some say not for the better.

What happens when it all goes wrong?
Case study: The Exxon Valdez

The fragile environment of Alaska can easily be upset. This was tragically demonstrated on March 24 1989, Good Friday, when the oil tanker *Exxon Valdez* spilled 11 million gallons of crude oil into Prince William Sound. The tanker had just loaded up in Valdez and was enroute for California. Soon after midnight on that fateful day, whilst trying to navigate through Prince William Sound, the tanker hit rocks and was holed below its water line. The ecological tragedy Alaska had been waiting for had finally happened. Some people said it would never happen – but it did.

The tragedy was particularly bad because:

- Prince William Sound was sheltered with only small waves, these did not break up the oil very well and so the oil could remain for years;
- the rocky coastline had many bays and coves, the total area affected was 800 miles;
- a 30 mph wind hampered the clean-up operation and caused the oil slick to travel further down Prince William Sound;
- there was a seven-hour delay in the rescue barge carrying the clean-up equipment, this meant more oil spilled into the sea.

Detergents are sprayed on the oil to try and disperse it

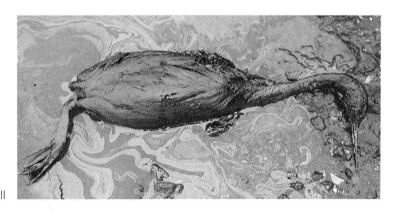

One victim of the oil spill

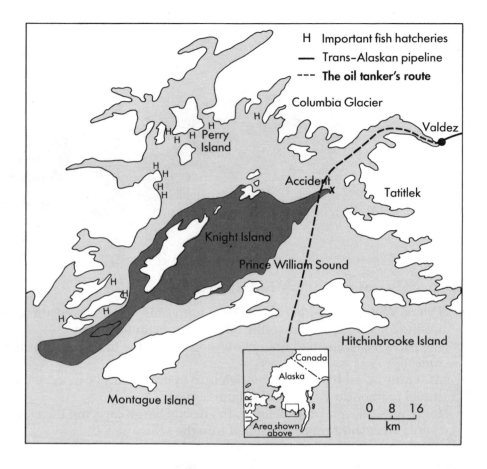

Spill Could Hit Alaska Wildlife for 10 years
by Roger Highfield, Science Editor

It could take 10 years for the Prince William Sound area to recover completely from the Alaskan oil spill disaster, experts said yesterday.

Exxon is assembling a team of marine biologists to evaluate the effects of the spill.

Facilities have been set up to treat oiled birds and mammals, such as otters, bears (which like to forage on the beach) and seals. Exxon is also working with local fishing interests to help identify and protect the most sensitive areas.

The body count is not what matters in calculations of the effect of the spill on the area. The crucial factor is the percentage of the local stock of each species that has been killed.

The season, speed of reproduction and movement of species from unaffected areas govern the recovery cycle.

Sea otters, migrating birds, herring and salmon are likely victims of the spill, according to one conservative group, the Defenders of Wildlife. The Sound is home to more than 20 000 sea otters, hundreds of sea lions and some killer whales.

Mr Rupert Cutler, president of the conservation group, said oil could destroy the insulating ability of the otters' fur and poison them when they eat oil-soaked fish.

'If the oil remains on the sea and the beaches for two more weeks, it could also kill millions of ducks, geese and shore birds which migrate through Prince William Sound.' Mr Cutler said.

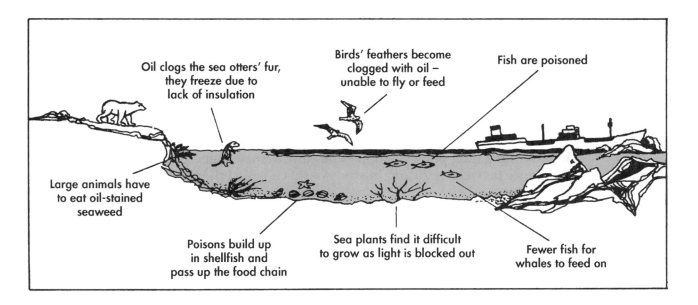

Oil clogs the sea otters' fur, they freeze due to lack of insulation

Birds' feathers become clogged with oil – unable to fly or feed

Fish are poisoned

Large animals have to eat oil-stained seaweed

Poisons build up in shellfish and pass up the food chain

Sea plants find it difficult to grow as light is blocked out

Fewer fish for whales to feed on

Now test yourself

Read the newspaper article on page 146.

12 Name:
(a) two fish (b) three birds (c) two other creatures which have been affected by the spill.

13 What will happen if sea otters' fur becomes soaked in oil?

14 Use your knowledge to explain why it will take ten years for the area's wildlife to recover.

15 In your opinion is it worth going to Alaska for oil? Give reasons for your answer.

Are there any alternatives to fossil fuels?
Case study: Tidal power in the Severn Estuary

Geothermal power

Wind power

Solar power

ALTERNATIVE ENERGY SOURCES

Tidal power

Biomass and dung

Hydro-electric power

Nuclear power

Using the power of the tides is a popular alternative source of energy. It works in this way:

- a barrier is built across the estuary;
- the barrier (or barrage) has gates (called sluice gates) which open and close along its length;
- the incoming or outgoing tide drives turbines as it flows through the gates;
- the turbines produce electricity.

In order for a tidal power station to produce sufficient energy there must be a big difference between high and low tides – this is called the **tidal range**.

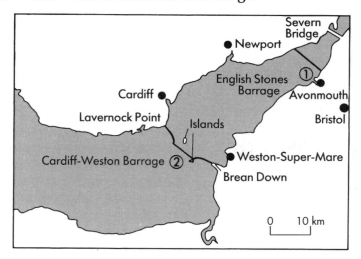

The two proposed barrage schemes

The Severn Estuary has the second largest tidal range in the world. The shape of the estuary is ideal. As the tide rushes in and out it is 'funnelled', so the energy is concentrated. After a 'feasibility study' by the Severn Tidal Power Group, two alternative schemes were suggested:

1   a small barrage near Avonmouth (English Stones Barrage);
2   a much larger barrage stretching from Cardiff to Weston (Cardiff-Weston Barrage).

The second barrage scheme has been recommended for development. It works in this way:

- sluice gates of the barrage open when the tide is coming in and close when high tide is reached, so that all the water is trapped behind the barrage;

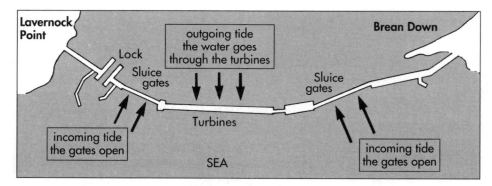

- the sluice gates remain closed as the sea is going out, instead the water rushes through the turbines and generates electricity;
- ships are allowed to pass through the barrage by special locks.

The barrage as a producer of electricity has its advantages:

- the electricity is cheaper and reliable;
- the Bristol Channel is dangerous for leisure activities at the moment, a barrage would make it safer;
- many jobs would be created for builders, engineers and power station staff;
- it would be a popular tourist attraction;
- more fish and birds would go to the quiet waters above the barrage;
- no harmful gases would be released into the atmosphere.

The Severn Estuary

The barrage also has its disadvantages:

- it will cost £6000 million to build;
- industrial waste and sewage presently dumped in the estuary would need costly treatment;
- power stations already using the estuary for cooling would have to change their systems;
- the Rivers Usk and Wye are important for salmon, and the mudflats along the estuary are important for wading birds, these would be threatened by the barrage;
- the ecological balance would be upset.

*L*evel Descriptions

At the start of Key Stage 3 the majority of pupils will have reached at least Level 4 in Geography. By the end of Key Stage 3 most pupils should be within the range of Levels 4–7. Levels 5–6 are the target for 14-year-olds. Level 8 is the standard reached by very able pupils.

Use our checklist to assess the Level reached, by ticking the skills that have been mastered.

Level 4

☐ Show knowledge, understanding and skills in relation to studies of a range of places and themes, at more than one scale.

☐ Begin to describe geographical patterns and to appreciate the importance of location in understanding places.

☐ Recognise and describe physical and human processes.

☐ Begin to show understanding of how these processes can change the features of places, and that these changes affect the lives and activities of people living there.

☐ Describe how people can both improve and damage the environment.

☐ Draw on knowledge and understanding to suggest suitable geographical questions for study.

☐ Use a range of geographical skills and evidence to investigate places and themes.

☐ Communicate findings using appropriate vocabulary.

Level 5

☐ Show knowledge, understanding and skills in relation to studies of a range of places and themes, at more than one scale

☐ Describe and begin to offer explanations for geographical patterns and for a range of physical and human processes.

☐ Describe how these processes can lead to similarities and differences between places.

☐ Describe ways in which places are linked through movements of goods and people.

☐ Offer explanations for ways in which human activities affect the environment and recognise that people attempt to manage and improve environments.

☐ Identify relevant geographical questions.

☐ Draw on knowledge and understanding to select and use appropriate skills and evidence to investigate places and themes.

☐ Reach plausible conclusions and present findings both graphically and in writing.

Level 6

- [ ] Show knowledge, understanding and skills in relation to a wide range of studies of places and themes, at various scales.
- [ ] Explain a range of physical and human processes.
- [ ] Describe ways in which processes operating at different scales create geographical patterns and lead to changes in places.
- [ ] Describe and offer explanations for different approaches to managing environments and appreciate that different approaches have different effects on people and places.
- [ ] Draw on knowledge and understanding to identify relevant geographical questions and suggest appropriate sequences of investigation.
- [ ] Select and make effective use of a wide range of skills and evidence in carrying out investigations.
- [ ] Present conclusions that are consistent with the evidence.

Level 7

- [ ] Show knowledge, understanding and skills in relation to a wide range of studies of places and themes, at various scales.
- [ ] Describe the interactions within and between physical and human processes.
- [ ] Show how these interactions create geographical patterns and contribute to change in places and patterns.
- [ ] Show understanding that many factors influence decisions made about places, and use this to explain how places change.
- [ ] Appreciate that peoples' lives and environment in one place are affected by actions and events in other places.
- [ ] Recognise that human actions may have unintended environmental consequences and that change sometimes leads to conflict.
- [ ] Draw on knowledge and understanding to identify geographical questions, establish a sequence of investigation, and select and use accurately a wide range of skills and evidence.
- [ ] Begin to reach substantiated conclusions.

Level 8

- [ ] Show knowledge, understanding and skills in relation to a wide range of studies of places and themes, at various scales.
- [ ] Offer explanations for interactions within and between physical and human processes.
- [ ] Explain changes over time in the characteristics of places.
- [ ] Begin to account for disparities in development and show some understanding of the range and complexity of factors that contribute to the quality of life in different places.
- [ ] Recognise the causes and consequences of environmental issues and show understanding of different approaches to tackling them.
- [ ] Understand and apply the concept of sustainable development.
- [ ] Draw on knowledge and understanding to identify appropriate geographical questions and implement an effective sequence of investigation.
- [ ] Select and use effectively and accurately a wide range of skills and evidence to reach substantiated conclusions.

Exceptional performance

☐ Show knowledge, understanding and skills in relation to studies of places and themes across the full range of scales.

☐ Explain complex interactions within and between physical and human processes.

☐ Explain and predict change over time in the characteristics of places.

☐ Show understanding of alternative approaches to development and the implications for the quality of life in different places.

☐ Assess the relative merits of different ways in which environmental issues are tackled and justify views about the different approaches.

☐ Understand and apply the concept of sustainable development in a range of contexts.

☐ Draw selectively on geographical ideas and theories, and use accurately a wide range of skills and evidence to undertake geographical enquiries independently at different scales.

☐ Reach substantiated conclusions and present them effectively and accurately.

☐ Evaluate work by suggesting improvements in approach and further lines of enquiry.

A nswers

Chapter 1

What is a map? page 8

1   Tim leaves his house in Brook Street and crosses Bailey Road near the park. He heads towards school. At the next junction, he turns left into Church Street. He walks along Church Street, passing the Dog and Duck pub and the church on his left and the public telephone on the other side of the road. At the traffic lights he turns left into Mary Street, crosses the road and visits the library. When he comes out of the library he turns left towards the traffic lights. At the junction he turns left into Church Street and heads towards the garage. At the junction he crosses the road to the shop, turns right and heads along Hawthorn Hill until he reaches John's house.

Scale and distance page 10

3   (a) Map C (b) Map A
4   St. Nicholas's (look at map A)
5   Reservoir and Iford Farm
6   Map C is drawn at too small a scale for such detail.

Measuring distance: page 11

7   (a) 2 km (b) 1.5 km (c) 750 m (d) 6 km
     (e) 2.5 km (f) 4.5 km (g) 700 m (h) 400 m
     (i) 550 m

Grid references: page 12

8   (a) Raleston (b) St. Harry (c) Short Park
     (d) Horse Bridge
9   (a) 0423 (b) 0420 (c) 0121 (d) 0124
10 (a) Church/Post office/Houses
     (b) School/Post office/Houses
11 (a) Farmhouse (b) Clubhouse (c) Farmhouse

Grid references: page 13

12			
⚐	Golf course	094145
⬙	Glasshouse	114144
♦	Church with steeple	084160
CH	Clubhouse	092153
⁜	Tumulus	104157
▪	Church with tower	115176
△	Triangulation pillar	115158
⚊	Windpump	088168
✕	Battlefield	095174
P	Post office	109162

Height on maps: page 14

14 A: Less than 10 m   B: 20 m
     C: 21–29 m   D: 31–38 m

Cross-sections: page 17

18 9399: steep   9597: flat   9395: gentle

Graphs: page 19

19 Pie chart   20 Scattergraph
21 Line graph   22 Bar graph

Map skills: pages 19–21

23 (a) 83 m (b) Whitley Batts (c) Chelwood Bridge
24 (a) East (b) Post office and church with tower
25 (a) Park Farm (b) Hunstrete Plantation
26 (a) Uphill (b) South
27 39 m
28 (a) right, then right again (b) about 10 km
29 Church, post office, houses
30 (a) 302140
     (b) 305136
     (c) 256145
     (d) 269118

31 (a) 2 km
     (b) 5 km
     (c) 6.5 km (straight-line bridge to bridge = 5.5 km)

32 (a) gently sloping
     (b) flat
     (c) steeply sloping

33 The village is Llanellen. The fare would be £4.50.

Chapter 2

Stephen's street: page 23

8   16
9   Ael-y-Bryn
10 No. Only residents and their visitors

The British Isles: page 25

15 (a) Belfast (b) Southampton (c) Glasgow and Edinburgh
16 (a) D5 (b) C4 (c) C5
17 C4
18 Newcastle upon Tyne
19 West
20 London

21 South-west, Bristol
22 Southampton

The British Isles: page 26
25 Grampians: Ben Nevis, 1347 m
Southern Uplands: Merrick, 843 m
Pennines: Cross Fell, 893 m
Lake District: Scafell, 978 m
Cambrian Mountains: Snowdon, 1085 m
Exmoor: Dunkery Beacon, 520 m
Dartmoor: Yes Tor, 618 m
26 Mersey: Pennines; Irish Sea. Clyde:
Southern Uplands; Irish Sea. Tyne: Cheviot
Hills; North Sea.
27 Shetlands; Orkneys; Scilly Isles; Outer
Hebrides; Inner Hebrides; Channel Islands

Chapter 3

Physical features of the world: page 30
3 Andes
4 An imaginary line in the Pacific Ocean;
when it is crossed a day is either gained or
lost
5 One day of the year receives 24 hours
daylight
6 (a) Pacific and Atlantic Oceans
(b) the Mediterranean and Red Seas

Economic development across the world:
page 33
12 (a) France (better food, hygiene, medicines,
more doctors per person)
(b) Few doctors; poverty, few hospitals
(c) Able to learn new skills; education
increases chances of getting jobs

Developed and developing countries: page 36
13 *Developed country*
Few employed in agriculture
Factories use machines, etc
Many employed in tertiary, etc
Farming is advanced, etc
Factory workers work for a set time, etc
Developing country
Many employed in agriculture
Factories need a lot of workers
Fewer employed in tertiary, etc
Farming is very primitive, etc
Factory workers work long hours, etc

Europe: page 36
14 (a) Austria, Belgium, Finland, Italy, Poland,
Spain
(b) **A** Athens, **B** Berlin, **L** Lisbon, **O** Oslo,
D Dublin, **K** Kiev
(c) **D** Danube, **R** Rhine

Chapter 4

France: page 37
1 1: English Channel 2: Bay of Biscay
3: Mediterranean
2 Corsica
3 Bordeaux, Lyons, Marseilles, Nantes
4 The Seine and the Rhone
5 I: Alps; II: Pyrenees; III: Massif Central

Contrasts in France: page 39
6 (a) Paris or French Riviera; (b) Massif
Central
7 Brittany: history, culture, beaches
Massif Central: mountain scenery
Paris: sights, shops
Alps: scenery, walks, mountains, winter
sports
French Riviera: sun, sea, beaches, climate
South-west: climate, beaches

Paris: page 40
8 It was a defensive site
9 (a) Government centre, roads and railways
meet there, TV and radio centre,
universities, industrial centre
(b) More young people moving to Paris;
fewer people left in the countryside; fewer
jobs there as industry is not attracted; rural
economy weak; traditional ways of life
threatened
10 1 Encourage more cars to be used, so
increasing noise and fumes
2 Would not really discourage people, as
many do not mind paying fines
3 Would create more congestion as people
look for parking spaces
4 Very drastic – would reduce economic
activity

Massif Central: page 41
11 Primitive, poor soils, steep slopes, harsh
climate
12 Highland area with steep slopes. No work
to attract people
13 (a) No jobs: no facilities for young; hard life
(b) "Bright lights", discos, bars, better
housing, job prospects
14 Maintain the economy, maintain the
culture, they do not want mass migration
15 Only occupied by owners during holiday
period – little money stays in area. Local
house prices forced up

Japan: page 43
16 (a) Hokkaido; Honshu; Kyushu; Shikoku
(b) Asia (c) Tokyo
17 Cassette players, CDs, TVs, videos, video
cameras, cameras

18 (b) Electrical goods, cameras, cars, etc
19 The need to import raw materials; mountainous interior
20 Commitment to work; workers are loyal to company; determination to succeed, etc

Imports and exports: page 45
21 Imports: goods brought into a country. Exports: goods sold to other countries. Balance of trade: the difference between imports and exports. Manufactured goods: things made in a factory.
22 Food; tea and coffee; fuels and minerals; chemicals
23 (a) Middle East; Indonesia (b) Japanese goods need lots of oil in their production
25 Countries gain wealth; some countries have goods which are not found elsewhere

Chapter 5

Bangladesh: page 47
1 (a) 1: Nepal 2: India 3: Burma 4: Bhutan 5: China (b) Bay of Bengal (c) Tropic of Cancer: $23\frac{1}{2}°N$
2 Many mouths to feed; problems may worsen in future; children need looking after
3 They are poor and must produce their own food. They cannot buy food and have no chance of other employment.

Bangladeshi family: page 50
6 (a) Father: farming, feeding oxen (b) Mother: cooking; washing up; looking after children; gathering firewood (c) Children: farming, firewood, washing clothes
7 The local stream
8 'The oxen are fed and watered'
9 Firewood

Hazards: page 51
10 It brings fertile mud and silt
11 A tropical storm
12 Water funnels up the Bay of Bengal, increasing the wave height.
13 Low-lying land; no warnings; primitive houses; lots of people in one small area; no medical facilities

Brazil: page 52
14 (a) 1: French Guiana; 2: Surinam; 3: Guyana; 4: Venezuela; 5: Colombia; 6: Bolivia; 7: Paraguay; 8: Argentina; 9: Uruguay; 10: Peru (b) A: Pacific Ocean; B: Atlantic Ocean (c) C: Equator; D: Tropic of Capricorn
15 Too young to work; need to be looked after; difficult to control population in future

16 Dense jungle, inaccessible

A country of contrasts: page 54
17 (In order) First paragraph: superb, businessman; coffee; exports; parties; drunk. Second paragraph: struggle; his best; shack; overcrowded; water; proper
18 South East Brazil
19 1: High class; 2: Low class/poverty line
20 There is tremendous wealth in Brazil but at the moment it is not distributed equally throughout the country

A typical Indian village: page 55
21 (a) 5 (b) 2 (c) 1 (d) 7 (e) 3 (f) 4 (g) 6 (h) 8 (i) 9
22 Wood: spears; bow and arrows; blowpipe; dug-out; housing frame. Grasses/reeds: fishing nets; roof; hammock

Changes in the Amazon rainforest: page 58
23 Dense forest
24 Deforestation; settlers moved in for agriculture and industry; roads built; land cleared
25 Road enables large machinery to be brought in
26 Need to bring in supplies of food
27 From farming and timber

Chapter 6

Plates: page 60
2 They are close to plate boundaries
3 Britain is not near a plate boundary. It is in a stable part of the world

Earthquake in Mexico: page 62
5 It happened during a 'rush hour'
6 Buildings collapsed, gas mains exploded, services were cut off
7 No light or water, no fuel, further tremors
8 The streets were covered in debris
9 500 miles (800 km)
10 It is built on stable rock

Chapter 7

The river story: page 66
2 Exmoor   3 B: Tiverton C: Exeter   4 Culm
5 English Channel   6 South

River processes: page 67
7 Loose material; a gentle slope gradually built up above river level
8 By its dark colour; build up of stones on the bed
9 Steep banks; undercutting

Hydrographs: page 76
10 A: Gentle rising limb; rural area; permeable rock
    B: Steep rising limb; urban area; impermeable rock
11 B: because the peak flow is higher than in A

Chapter 8

Hydrological cycle: page 78
1 Ocean (1); Plants (2) Groundwater (3); Atmosphere (4); Snow and ice (5); Rivers and lakes (6); Precipitation (A); Transpiration (B); Condensation (C); Throughflow (D); Run off (E); Evaporation (F)

Reservoirs: page 80
2 (a) Chairman (b) Local resident (c) Water Company Manager (d) Conservationist (e) Farmer (f) Watersports enthusiast
3 For: chairman, water company manager, watersports enthusiast. Against: farmer, local resident, conservationist.
4 Narrow valleys are easy to dam; deep, so they hold a lot of water; mountains have few people living there and heavy rainfall
5 Water meters; public awareness; 'Save it' campaigns; advertisements; water-efficient appliances

Dirty water: page 82
6 (In order) Acid rain; Sewage disposal; Nitrates; Farmyard slurry; Landfill seepage; Factory discharges; Power stations; Traffic fumes

North Sea: page 83
8 1. England 2. Scotland 3. Norway
   4. Denmark 5. Germany 6. The Netherlands
   7. Belgium 8. France

Chapter 9

Weather and climate: page 86
1 (a) Windy conditions bring dangerous waves
   (b) Storms at sea can threaten boats
   (c) Frosts may kill young, tender plants
   (d) People do not shop as much in bad weather

Microclimates: page 86
3 1:24°C 2: 26°C 3: 19.4°C 4: 22°C 5: 21°C
4 (a) site 2; (b) site 3 5 Site 3
6 Site 1 is quite warm, due to its tarmac playground; 2 is sheltered from the wind, so is warm; 3 is exposed to the cooling breeze; 4 is sheltered by trees; 5 is not in the shade and is on a grassy surface

Weather in Britain: page 88
8 (a) False (b) True (c) True (d) False
9 W: Blackpool; X: Pembroke; Y: Inverness; Z: Bournemouth
10 (a) During July temperatures decrease south to north. Coleraine is further north, so cooler. During January temperatures decrease west to east, away from the influence of the Atlantic Ocean. Coleraine is closer to the warmer ocean
    (b) It is more inland and furthest south, so quickly warms up
    (c) A huge curve around the Irish Sea – the sea is warmer than the land during January

High pressure: page 91
11 Similarities: clear skies; sunshine. Differences: very cold, foggy in winter; warm and sunny in summer
12 Wind strength and direction, pressure

Low pressure: page 92
14 A warm front passing over
15 The move from cold to warm to cold sectors of the depression
16 It moves anticlockwise around a depression – as the depression moves, the wind direction changes

Weather vs. climate: page 93
20 Above average – shown by more red on the graph than blue.

Climate change: page 95
21 All – except Mexico City and Paris.
22 Firth of Forth; Teesside; Humberside; Norfolk Broads; Thames Valley; Severnside.
23 Do not use cars so much; use energy more efficiently; use paper wisely, so trees are not unnecessarily cut down; recycle as much waste as possible

Chapter 10

Savanna: page 98
1 They have thick outer skins; they store water
2 The lower the latitude the denser the vegetation

Chapter 11

Egypt: population: page 100
1 57 people per square km
2 Sparse, except near the River Nile
3 The people are all in one area

4   Mountainous; desert
5   Near water supply, lowland; the river means food can be grown

Birth and death rates: pages 100–101
8   (a) 1921; (b) It would decrease
9   Differences: higher birth and death rates; greater total population; greater rate of natural increase in Bangladesh. Similarities: population increasing; death rates fell initially

Population change: page 102
10 Little change; rapid increase; rapid decrease

Size of families: page 102
11 Children are expensive to bring up; women want to pursue careers; family planning, etc
12 They help produce food; it is the custom; they will look after parents when they are older, etc
13 It is low in developing countries

Reasons for moving: page 103
14 A forced move: fear of persecution; famine; disease; war; possibly promotion
    Choice: new house; friends and relatives; marriage; retirement; attractive areas; possibly promotion

Ernie Martin: page 104
16 (a) Five (b) Three

Kurds: page 105
19 Turkey, Syria, Iran, Iraq
20 Arrows point to Iran and Turkey
21 War
22 Lack of food; cold; poor hygienic conditions; exhaustion, etc
23 Threat of losing their lives

Chapter 12

Settlements: page 107
2   Dry point: B; Gap: C; Defensive: D; Wet point: A; Bridging point: E
3   (a) E: all roads should lead there; D: Defensive reasons

Settlement patterns: page 109
4   Nucleated: C; Dispersed: B; Linear: A
5   The crossroads
6   It is confined by a narrow valley
7   Farmers

Town functions: page 110
8   A, B and C: Industry; D: Administration centre; E: Port; F: Market centre; G: Resort
9   (a) B (b) C (c) A
10 D: All roads lead there; it is easier to get to

11 G: It is a tourist area
12 F: It is a farming community
13 D: Need to be near roads; it is the largest settlement, with more people

Minehead: pages 113–114
15 (a) More housing; better trade possibilities – more tourists; an eyesore disappears
    (b) Yes! Increased tourist traffic in summer, but who will benefit – local traders or the holiday company?

Cardiff Bay: page 117
20 Danger to wildlife; flooding; break up of communities; water quality
21 It will clean up the area; clean the rivers; if not here, then other environments would be destroyed

Too much traffic!: page 119
24 Description of line graph: Peaks during rush hours when many people going to and from work or school. Little traffic during early hours when they are asleep.

Are there solutions?: page 120
26 More: (a) (c) (h) (j) Less: (b) (d) (e) (f) (g) (i)

Where to build a by-pass: page 121
27 1: Goes through farmland
    2: Golf course affected
    3: Hills and woods affected
28 Route 2 is better – it is shorter and would affect a smaller area than the other suggested routes

Chapter 13

Competition for land: page 122
1   Large: farm; golf course; airport; industrial complex; motorway. Small: sports centre; house; shoe shop
2   (a) and (d)

Mr Meadmore's farm: page 125
3   Cheese; milk; butter; yoghurt, etc
4   Too far for them to walk
5   (a) Growing a different crop in each field every year
    (b) It allows fields to regain their fertility

Industry in South Wales: page 127
7   They needed coal and iron ore from the local area, and a supply of limestone
8   The products which go to make something in a factory
9   The need to import raw materials; cheap land available
10 Very expensive to run a steelworks; fall in demand for steel products

South Wales: page 128

11 All are near a motorway for transport services and near major towns for workforce needs

Shoe shops: page 128

12 Shop 1: it is closest to the car park

13 No: you like to compare prices and styles

14 Shop 5: it is furthest from the car park

Superstores: page 129

15 Cheap petrol; easy parking

16 Lorries need large areas to turn – they do not disturb shoppers this way

17 No, a free bus is provided

18 Easy for deliveries, easy for shoppers to get there

Tourism in Europe: page 130

19 Travel agents, tour operator, coach driver, pilot, flight attendant, courier, waitress, bar staff, etc

22 Portugal, Spain, France, Italy, Greece, Britain. Attractions of the Mediterranean and its climate

23 Too cold

Holidays in Britain: page 131

24 Fine beaches; warmer, drier summers

25 Centre of British tradition; many sights to see; theatres

26 Families: all-round entertainment – something to do on wet days

27 Any (give valid reasons)

Holidays in the sun: page 134

28 Mediterranean/Aegean

29 Beaches; climate; traditional Greek food; culture

31 Electricity; jobs provided; hotels built; marina built; new roads built, marshes drained, etc

Winter resorts: page 135

32 Winter resorts are increasing in popularity

33 (a) An activity that needs special training equipment and facilities (b) A prepared area for skiing (c) Evening entertainment

34 (a) It is guaranteed to have snow (b) Skiers need snow!

35 Deforestation; compact soil; ski lifts use up land; many people are attracted to an environmentally sensitive area – pressure on scarce resources

National Parks: page 138

NPA – National Parks Authority

NPO – National Parks Officer

LO – Landowners

V – Visitors

B – Building

CP – Caravan Parks

C – Campsite

D – Dulverton

HaC – Hikers and Climbers

CC – Countryside Code

G – Gates

CW – Conservation Work

FaB – Footpaths and Bridleways

L – Litter

EF – Exhaust Fumes

PS – Picnic Site

H – Houses

SaC – Sheep and Cattle

Chapter 14

The Earth's resources: page 140

1 Renewable: fish, timber, wheat, cotton; Non-renewable: coal, iron ore

2 Exhausted: run out; reserves: what is left in the earth; recycling: using each product more than once; resources: valuable materials; manufactured goods: something that is made; raw materials: things needed to make something

3 Cod: fish finger; Iron ore: rail; Gold: ring; Wool: sweater; Timber: table; Clay: brick

Oil in Alaska: page 144

9 More profit is made than costs incurred

10 Frozen ground; wildlife; darkness; severe cold; earthquakes

11 High wages; holiday benefits

Alaskan wildlife: page 147

12 (a) Herring, salmon (b) Ducks, geese, shore birds (c) Otters, bears, seals

13 They will freeze to death

14 Fragile environment; very harsh climate, etc

Glossary

Abrasion A form of erosion where rocks rub against other rocks.

Accessibility How easy a place is to get to.

Acid rain Rainwater mixed with gases, produced when fossil fuels are burnt.

Agriculture Farming the land and producing food.

Algal bloom Large amounts of algae found in the sea.

Alluvium Fertile mud spread by a river during flood.

Alternative energy Energy resources other than fossil fuels.

Amenities Places of relaxation and enjoyment

Antarctic Circle An imaginary line around the Earth of a latitude of 66$\frac{1}{2}$°S.

Anticyclone A high pressure weather system.

Arable farming The growing of crops.

Arctic Circle An imaginary line around the Earth at a latitude of 66$\frac{1}{2}$°N.

Ash Material that comes out of a volcano during an eruption.

Assembly plant A factory where lots of different parts are put together to make a finished product.

Atlas A book containing maps of the world.

Atmosphere The gases that surround the Earth.

Attrition A form of erosion where two rock particles rub together.

Balance of trade The difference between imports and exports.

Barrage An artificial wall built across a bay or a river.

Base flow The usual amount of water flowing in a river.

Bay An inlet found at the coast.

Beach Sand or pebbles deposited along a coast.

Biological weathering The breakdown of rocks by plants and animals.

Birth rate The number of people being born per year.

Blowhole A hole on a cliff above the sea, from which air escapes.

Bore hole A hole dug deep into the ground to find water.

Bridging point The easiest place to build a bridge across a river.

Business park A collection of businesses and factories in one place.

Buttress A large root found in trees in the rainforest.

By-pass A road built around a town.

Canopy The continuous layer of tops of trees found in the rainforest.

Capital The amount of money needed for any venture.

Capital city Usually the most important city in a country – where the centre of government is found.

Cavitation Erosion caused by bubbles in fast-flowing streams.

Central business district The commercial centre of the town.

Channel The part of the land in which a river is found.

Chemical weathering The breakdown of rocks by acids in rainwater.

City A large town with many services.

Cliff A steep or sheer rock face.

Climate The average weather of a particular place.

Cold front Where cold air meets warmer air.

Commercial The buying and selling of goods or services.

Communications The ease with which people and goods can move from place to place.

Community A group living together.

Comparison goods Goods where people can compare prices and styles.

Composite cone A volcano made up of alternate layers of ash and lava.

Condensation Water droplets form as a result of a drop in temperature.

Congestion A build-up of traffic, usually in a town.

Conservation Looking after the environment.

Continent A large land mass made up of a number of countries.

Contour line A line joining places of the same height above sea level.

Contour pattern Groups of contour lines showing the shape of the land.

Convectional rainfall Rainfall caused through warm air rising from a warm surface.

Corrasion Erosion caused by pebbles rubbing against solid rock.

Corrosion Erosion resulting from chemical change.

Country The land that is run by a particular government.
County A small part of a country.
Course The path a river takes.
Crop rotation Growing different crops in the same field each year.
Cross-section A way of showing the shape of the land.

Dairy farming Producing milk and milk products.
Dam A wall built to keep back water.
Death rate The number of people who die per year.
Defensive site The place chosen for a settlement that is easy to protect from attack.
Derelict land Waste ground which was once built on.
Deposition The gradual build up of pebbles, sand and small particles of rock.
Depression A low pressure weather system.
Developed country A wealthy country which has developed its resources.
Developing country A poor country which is trying to develop its resources.
Direction Shown on a map by a compass.
Discharge The amount of water in a river.
Drought A long period without rainfall.

Earthquake A violent shaking of the Earth's crust.
Eastings Shown on a map as the vertical lines of a grid.
Economic growth How quickly a country is increasing its wealth and raising living standards.
Economic output The total amount of goods coming out of a factory or a country.
Economically viable Where the profits made are greater than the costs incurred.
Emigrant A person who moves away from a town or country.
Emergents The largest trees of the forest.
Employment The number of people who have jobs.
Environment The places where people live.
Epicentre The point on the Earth's surface where an earthquake occurs.
Epiphyte One plant growing on another plant.
Equator An imaginary line around the Earth at latitude 0°.
Erosion The natural wearing away of rocks.
Eruption When a volcano throws out rock, ash, lava and gas.
European Community A group of twelve European countries.
Evaporation Water changing from a liquid to a gas as a result of being warmed.
Exports Goods being sold to other countries.

Factory A building where things are made.
Farm A piece of land where crops are grown or animals are kept for food.
Farming Producing food on a farm.
Fertile soil A soil which is good for growing things in.
Fertiliser Substances that help crops to grow.
Fetch How far a wave has travelled.
Fieldwork Gathering data outside the classroom.
Finished product A complete article from a factory that can now be sold.
Flood Water covering land that is usually dry.
Flood plain The flat area of land next to a river.
Flood risk Whether or not it is likely that a flood will occur.
Fossil fuels Fuels that are burnt, e.g., gas, coal and oil.
Focus The exact point within the Earth where an earthquake takes place.
Freeze-thaw action Repeated freezing and thawing.
Freight Goods that are being transported from one place to another.
Fresh water Non-salty water, found on the land.
Frontal rainfall Rain occurring as a result of warm air meeting cold air.
Function The main purpose of a town.

Gap town A town formed between two hills.
Glacier A river of ice.
Goods Items that people use.
Gorge A very steep-sided valley.
Grants Money given by the government for a specific purpose.
Greenhouse effect The heat from the Earth not allowed to escape back into space.
Grid Lines on a map.
Grid reference A way of finding places on a map quickly and accurately.
Gross national product The total value of all goods and services produced by a country in a year.
Groundwater Water in the rocks underground.
Groyne A wall on a beach built at right angles to the coastline.

Hamlet A small village.
Headland A rocky piece of land sticking out into the sea.
Hierarchy Shops grouped together according to size and importance.

High pressure A weather system which usually brings clear skies.

High tide When the tide is furthest inland.

High water mark The level reached by high tide.

Home market Goods produced for, and sold in, this country.

Housing estate A collection of modern houses.

Humus Dead and decaying leaves and other parts of plants.

Hydraulic action A form of erosion where water squeezes air into cracks.

Hydro-electric power Power generated by using water.

Hydrograph A graph showing the relationship between the amount of rainfall and the amount of water in a river.

Hydrological cycle The path water takes from the sea, to air, to land, to sea.

Ice sheet A large expanse of ice found in high latitudes.

Immigrant Someone who has moved into a country from another country.

Impermeable Something through which water will not pass.

Imports Goods brought into a country from abroad.

Income How much a person or a country earns.

Industry The term used to describe the production of goods and the generation of wealth.

Industrial estate An area of land where several factories can be found.

Infant mortality The number of babies who die before their first birthday.

Infertile soil Soil that is no good for growing crops.

Inner city The old industrial area next to the city centre.

Interlocking spurs Fingers of land around which a river winds itself.

International Date Line An imaginary line at about 180° of longitude. Every time you cross it the date changes.

International trade The exchange of goods and services between the countries of the world.

Irrigation The moving of water to grow crops.

Island An area of land surrounded by water.

Isobar A line joining places of the same pressure.

Isotherm A line joining places of the same average temperature.

Key Usually found on a map, a line of symbols and their meanings.

Lag A time delay.

Landfall sites Huge holes in the ground where domestic rubbish is dumped.

Latitude Imaginary, parallel lines running from east to west across the Earth.

Lava Rock which comes out of a volcano.

Leeward The side of a hill facing away from the wind.

Leisure Spare time.

Ley grass Grass that is planted.

Lianas Long, thin, rapidly-growing plants found in the rainforest.

Life expectancy How long people are expected to live.

Linear A straight-line pattern.

Literacy rates How many people can read and write.

Load The amount of rocky material in a river.

Local area The area surrounding your house or school.

Longitude Imaginary lines running around the Earth from the North Pole to the South Pole.

Longshore drift The way in which pebbles and sand are moved along the coast by the sea.

Low pressure A weather system that usually brings cloud and rain.

Low tide When the tide is furthest out to sea.

Low water mark The level of low tide.

Magma Collective name for all material thrown out by a volcano.

Magma chamber Where magma is stored before a volcanic eruption.

Manufactured goods Products that are made in factories.

Manufacturing Making things in a factory.

Map A drawing of a place or area.

Market The place where goods are sold.

Meander A large bend in a river.

Microclimate The weather of a very small area.

Migrant Someone who has moved home.

Migration The act of moving home.

Mixed farming Farming by growing crops and keeping animals.

Mouth Where a river ends.

National park A protected area of outstanding natural beauty.

National Rivers Authority The organisation that has responsibility for keeping rivers clean.

Natural features Not artificial.

Natural hazard A natural threat to life, e.g. volcano, earthquake or flood.

Natural increase A population term used to describe the difference between birth rates and death rates.

Natural resources Things of value found in nature.

Network A series of roads or railways linked together.
Non-renewable resources Resources that will run out one day.
Northings Shown on a map as the horizontal lines of a grid.
Notch A small area at the base of a cliff eroded by the sea.
Nucleated Centred around one place.

Ocean A large expanse of sea.
Ordnance Survey The organisation that produces Ordnance Survey maps.
Organic farming Farming without using artificial chemicals and fertilisers.
Organic material Plant and animal remains.
Overhang The part of a waterfall that will eventually collapse.

Parasites Plants and insects that feed on other living organisms.
Parent material The original rock from which a soil forms.
Passengers People who are travelling.
Pastoral farming The farming of animals.
Permanent pasture Grassland that is never ploughed up.
Permeable Something through which water passes easily.
Petrol-chemicals Chemicals produced from oil.
Physical map A map showing natural features, such as mountains and rivers.
Physical weathering The breakdown of rocks into smaller and smaller particles.
Pie graph A circular graph, usually used to show percentages.
Plan view A view from directly above.
Plain A flat piece of land.
Plate A solid section of the Earth's crust.
Plate tectonics The study of how the Earth's plates move.
Political map A map showing countries, counties, towns and cities.
Pollution Things that can harm the environment, e.g. chemicals, dirt and noise.
Population The total number of people in an area.
Population density The number of people living in a specific area.
Port Where goods are brought into and sent out of the country.
Poverty Very low standards of living.
Precipitation All water which falls from the sky as rain, snow, hail, etc.
Prevailing wind The direction from which the wind normally blows.

Primary activity The extraction of natural resources.
Prime meridian An imaginary line of longitude 0°, running through Greenwich, from the North Pole to the South Pole.

Questionnaire A list of questions designed to ask people their opinions on a subject.

Rainforest The dense, jungle lands of the world.
Rain shadow An area which does not receive much rain, due to being protected by a mountain.
Ratio The proportion of one variable to another.
Reclaimed land An area of land which was once under the sea.
Recreation A pleasurable interest or activity enjoyed during spare time.
Recycling Using products more than once.
Redevelopment Modernising areas of land that have become derelict.
Region An area of a country.
Relief The shape of the land.
Relief rainfall Rainfall found on mountains where air is forced to rise.
Renewable resources Resources that will never run out.
Reserves A supply of resources which could be used in the future.
Reservoir An area of stored water.
Resident Someone who lives in an area.
Resort A town that specialises in providing holidays.
Resources Things that are useful to people.
Richter scale A scale used to measure earthquake intensity.
Ridge A long, narrow hill.
Route The path taken on a journey.
Run off Water moving across the Earth's surface.
Rural In the countryside.

Saltation A way in which small particles jump downstream.
Salt marsh An area of land where sea water becomes stagnant.
Sanitation Related to the disposal of human waste.
Savanna Large areas of grassland.
Scale The link between the distance measured on a map and its true distance in reality.
Secondary activity The making of goods in a factory (same as manufacturing).
Seismograph An instrument used to show the intensity of an earthquake.

Services An economic activity where nothing is produced, but a person's skill is paid for.
Settlement A collection of buildings where people live.
Sewage sludge Produced by human waste.
Shock waves A series of tremors occurring after an earthquake.
Silage Green grass that is cut, sealed and kept for winter feed.
Silt Small particles of mud found in a river.
Site The place where a town or a factory is located.
Sketch map A rough drawing of a place.
Sluice gate A gate which controls the flow of water through a barrage or lock.
Slurry Farmyard waste.
Social conditions People's standard of living.
Soil erosion The washing away of the soil.
Soil texture The size of the particles making up the soil.
Solar radiation Heat and light received from the sun.
Solution Chemicals that are dissolved in water.
Source The start of a stream.
Spit A pebble or sand deposit found along the coastline.
Spot height The height of a specific place as shown on a map.
Stack A piece of rock found along the coast where erosion is occurring.
Storm flow The extra height of the high tide as a result of a storm.
Storm surge The extra amount of water in a river as a result of a storm.
Stream A small river.
Suburbs The residential areas found on the edge of a town or city.
Succulents Plants that are adapted to living in desert conditions by storing water.
Superstore A large shop selling most household items and food.
Suspension Material held within the main body of a river.

Tertiary activity Providing services.
Throughflow Water flowing through the soil and rocks.
Tidal range The difference between the highest and lowest tides.
Tidal wave A huge wave resulting from a storm or an earthquake.
Tourist Someone who visits an area for recreational purposes.
Town A large collection of buildings.
Traction Material being rolled along the bed of a river.

Transpiration Water given off by plants.
Transport The movement of people, goods and other materials from one place to another.
Treatment works Where domestic water supplies are cleaned.
Tributary A small river joining a larger one.
Tropic of Cancer An imaginary line of latitude at $23^1/_2°$N.
Tropic of Capricorn An imaginary line of latitude at $23^1/_2°$S.
Tsunami A tidal wave.
Tube well A way of obtaining water in dry countries.
Turbines Blades which rotate with moving water.
Typhoon A tropical storm.

Undercutting Erosion eating away at the base of a cliff.
Undergrowth Vegetation lying on the surface under the tree layer.
Urban Towns and cities.
Urbanisation The rapid growth of towns and cities.

Valley The low ground between two hills.
Vegetation The plants of an area.
Village A small settlement.
Volcanic eruptions Periods when a volcano is giving off steam, lava, gas and solid particles.

Warm front A place where warm air is forced to rise above colder air.
Water cycle The path water takes from the sea, to the air, to the land, and back to the sea.
Waterfall A point in a river where water falls vertically for a distance.
Wave-cut platform A flat area of coastline where cliffs have been eroded.
Wave refraction The bending of waves in the sea.
Weathering The breakdown of rocks by the weather.
Weather satellite A piece of machinery in space which sends information about the Earth's atmosphere.
Wind The movement of air.
Windward The side of the mountain directly facing the wind.
World Bank The organisation to which poor countries apply for loans.

Yield How much is produced from a set area of land.

I ndex